Growing
Global Digital
Citizens

Better Practices That Build Better Learners

Lee Watanabe Crockett
Andrew Churches

Solution Tree | Press

a division of

Solution Tree

555 North Morton Street
Bloomington, IN 47404
800.733.6786 (toll free) / 812.336.7700
FAX: 812.336.7790
email: info@SolutionTree.com
SolutionTree.com

Visit **go.SolutionTree.com/technology** to download the free reproducibles in this book.

Printed in the United States of America

21 20 19 18 17   1 2 3 4 5

Library of Congress Cataloging in Publication Data

Names: Crockett, Lee, author. | Churches, Andrew, author.

Title: Growing global digital citizens : better practices that build better
  learners / Lee Watanabe Crockett, Andrew Churches.

Description: Bloomington, IN : Solution Tree Press, [2017] | Includes
  bibliographical references and index.

Identifiers: LCCN 2017013962 | ISBN 9781945349119 (perfect bound)

Subjects: LCSH: International education. | World citizenship--Study and
  teaching. | Education--Effect of technological innovations on. | Education
  and globalization.

Classification: LCC LC1090 .C75 2017 | DDC 370.116--dc23 LC record available at https://lccn.loc.
gov/2017013962

Solution Tree

Jeffrey C. Jones, CEO
Edmund M. Ackerman, President

Solution Tree Press

President and Publisher: Douglas M. Rife
Editorial Director: Sarah Payne-Mills
Managing Production Editor: Caroline Cascio
Senior Production Editor: Todd Brakke
Senior Editor: Amy Rubenstein
Copy Editor: Evie Madsen
Proofreader: Elisabeth Abrams
Text and Cover Designer: Abigail Bowen
Editorial Assistants: Jessi Finn and Kendra Slayton

Acknowledgments

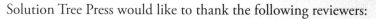

Solution Tree Press would like to thank the following reviewers:

Keith Crowley
Principal and Associate Head of School
St. John's Preparatory School
Danvers, Massachusetts

Chris Herzfeld
Principal
Laguna Beach High School
Laguna Beach, California

Mike Jasso
Principal
Coppell High School
Coppell, Texas

Scott Simmons
Director of Curriculum, Technology, and
    Assessment
Northwestern School Corporation
Kokomo, Indiana

Nate Simons
Technology Director
Logan-Magnolia Community Schools
Logan, Iowa

You Are a Global Digital Citizen

Your identity transcends geographical and political borders.

Humankind is one, and it is full of love. Embrace this great community.

Help where there is true need, and cooperate to make change permanent.

Be compassionate.

Have your own ideas and express them, and be open to new ways of seeing or being.

Be mindful. Your actions transcend time and space, touching everyone and everything.

Respect and take responsibility for yourself, others, and everything around you.

Stay curious and learn about the world.

Look after your environment.

Be mindful of what you need, what you take, and how you use it.

Believe you can make a positive difference.

Take action to fix problems, resolve issues, and overcome challenges to achieve results you believe to be honest, just, and fair for yourself and for humankind alike.

Be your best self by lifting others to be their best selves.

—Lee Watanabe Crockett

Table of Contents

Reproducible pages are in italics.

Chapter 6

Developing the Wider Community **83**

Chapter 7

Growing Global Digital Citizenship **99**

Appendix A

Global Matters **107**

Appendix B

Appendix C

Visit **go.SolutionTree.com/technology** to
download the free reproducibles in this book.

About the Authors

Lee Watanabe Crockett is an optimist. He believes in a bright future and our ability to build it together through connection and compassion. He is an author, a speaker, a designer, an inspirational thinker, and the creative mind behind some of the most exciting transformations in worldwide education. In life, Lee believes in creating balance in the reality of a digital present and future. As such, he has cultivated skills in aikido, studied the traditional tea ceremony while living in Japan, and studied painting in Italy. He also studies traditional Buddhist music, which he performs on a *shakuhachi*, a Japanese bamboo flute.

Lee is curious about life and the shared human experience. This curiosity is infectious, as anyone who has heard Lee speak can tell you. Joyful curiosity is the foundation of his approach to creating healthy learning environments for groups around the world.

Lee is coauthor of *Mindful Assessment*, *Understanding the Digital Generation*, *The Digital Diet*, *Living on the Future Edge*, and the bestseller *Literacy Is Not Enough*. He works with educators and corporations in several countries, helping them make the shift to regain relevance and establish a culture of excellence.

To learn more about Lee's work, visit https://globaldigitalcitizen.org or www .leewatanabecrockett.com, or follow @leecrockett on Twitter.

Andrew Churches is a teacher and an information and communication technology enthusiast. He teaches at Kristin School, a school with a mobile computing program that teaches students with personal mobile devices and laptops, on the North Shore of Auckland, New Zealand.

Andrew is also an edublogger, a wiki author, and an innovator. In 2008, Andrew's wiki, *Educational Origami*, was nominated for the Edublog Awards' Best Educational Wiki award. He contributes to several websites and blogs, including *Tech & Learning* magazine, *Spectrum Education* magazine, and *The Committed Sardine Blog*. Andrew believes that to prepare students for the future, we must prepare them for change and teach them to question, think, adapt, and modify.

He is the coauthor of *Mindful Assessment, The Digital Diet, Apps for Learning*, and the bestseller *Literacy Is Not Enough*.

To learn more about Andrew's work, visit https://globaldigitalcitizen.org, or follow @achurches on Twitter.

To book Lee Watanabe Crockett or Andrew Churches for professional development, contact pd@SolutionTree.com.

Introduction

Lee's mother was in her sixties when she told him she regretted never visiting Paris. She had secretly always dreamed of going, but during her life had never been outside North America. In 2005, over a cup of coffee, Lee slid two tickets to Paris across the table, and a few weeks later, she ate a crepe late at night under the Eiffel Tower. He had never seen her happier. It was a very special trip, and this city, which he had visited many times before and knew well, repeatedly showed them its beauty and graciousness.

On the morning they planned to go to the Louvre, she was impatient and anxious as they lingered over the normal French breakfast of coffee and croissants. She told him she wanted to get an early start so she could see everything before it got busy—Lee felt the need to manage expectations and frame the experience a little. He gently told her the Louvre is one of the largest museums in the world. There are well over seventy thousand artworks in its sprawling 650,000 square feet of gallery space. There are over eight million visitors a year, so they could expect to share it with twenty-two thousand people that day. But even if they were by themselves and only spent thirty seconds in front of each work of art, it would take almost six hundred hours to see it all—it's just not possible in a day. Instead, he suggested they take their time, decide then on the few things she really wanted to see, and then gaze at anything that caught their eyes in between, letting the crowds rush past as they wandered.

At the top of her list was the *Mona Lisa*, and as they got close, the crowd got thicker and more aggressive. Lee will always remember this moment. A security guard saw him trying to protect her from being knocked over and stepped forward to assist. The guard stopped the crowd and moved them back, taking his mother on his arm and escorting her directly in front of Leonardo da Vinci's masterpiece. He paused and said to her, "Take all the time you like, madame. There is no rush. Enjoy this moment completely." She did just that and gazed in wonder. Lee was so happy that he had studied painting in Florence because he was able to answer her questions and provoke her curiosity. It was as magical as watching a child discover his or her own hands.

As they stood there, Lee noticed many people funnel past, snapping a quick photo, and moving on. Most never saw the painting except through their camera lenses. He often recalls thinking how strange it was to spend the time and money to get to Paris just to take a picture and not even stop to look.

This was before the smartphone and long before the selfie. Now a visit to the museum means dodging not only the crowds but also trying to ignore the constant flashes and fake camera click sounds and, worst of all, navigating the sea of selfie sticks patrons precariously wave around.

Speaking of smartphones, did you check yours in the last hour? How about your email? Maybe you've updated your Facebook status or pinned something today? Are you following us on Twitter (@leecrockett and @achurches)? How are those LinkedIn connections doing? Have you texted anyone, checked your steps, looked at the weather, watched a video, played a game, logged your workout, recorded your food, or spent time searching for a productivity app that will help you get on top of your life?

People with smartphones and a data plan now hold access to the sum total of human knowledge and history in the palms of their hands. ScienceDaily reports that 90 percent of all online data in the world was generated between 2011 and 2013 (SINTEF, 2013). In light of this, is it any wonder our education institutions are grappling with how to affirm their purpose? It used to be that when someone posed a question in a social situation, discourse ensued, opinions and assumptions flew, and everyone was engaged in rich dialogue. Now it seems that the inevitable outcome of asking a question in a group will be the competition to see who can look it up fastest, followed by blank looks at each other with nothing left to talk about, and then everyone looking back to his or her phones for some sort of stimulation. Someone once told Lee the story of how, in this setting, as he grabbed his phone to verify his position, someone reached across and gently covered his phone and asked, "Would it be all right if, for just a little while, we didn't know and could just wonder about it?" Wouldn't it be marvelous if we all gave ourselves permission to *wonder* instead of *know*? Just for a few moments? Imagine the possibilities that could arise from being curious.

In February 2017, Facebook projected it would cross two billion monthly active users by mid-year (Popper & Erlick, 2017), which it did (Welch, 2017)—and Facebook is only one of hundreds of social networking opportunities. We have never been more connected than we are today, and yet for so many, we have never felt more alone. The Nike run app will stream your running route to your Facebook wall in real time, and your friends can cheer you on—literally. They click a button on your post, and you hear a crowd roaring on your phone with a message saying who cheered you on. This is really cool, but most people would rather their friends were with them on the run—that they were talking to each other, changing the pace and the route, and encouraging each other at the moment they actually needed it.

It doesn't have to be this way. And, no, you don't have to give up your modern-day conveniences. Yes, devices can keep people distracted and isolated from engaging fully in life, but they also can be tools to help us to learn from each other and to change the world. It's a question of how we use them. It's a question of *global digital citizenship.*

Technology provides some of the biggest teachable moments ever. Through this book, we will share what we've learned through our experiences working with hundreds of schools around the world. We will help you transform acceptable use policies, restrictions, and outright bans to a system of cultivating respect and responsibility for oneself, others, and everything around us. We will show you how to expand the process to grow responsible, ethical, global citizens in a digital world.

Digital Citizenship Versus Global Digital Citizenship

When Internet-connected technology first started to appear in schools, educators quickly realized the need for guidelines for acceptable use of that technology. This most often resulted in restrictive *acceptable use policies* that often didn't serve students' needs or guide behavior outside the classroom. In this book, we discuss the limitations of these policies, which are primarily a list of rules and regulations rather than a guiding set of principles students can live throughout their lives.

Digital citizenship describes how a person should behave in the online world. Frequently, when schools create policies and programs around digital citizenship, they are primarily the content of an acceptable use policy enhanced with an educational component that focuses heavily on protecting students from online predation and cyberbullying.

Global citizenship is a well-understood concept relating to how one participates in and contributes to the world as a whole. What then is *global digital citizenship,* and how does it connect online behavior to one's participation in the global community?

Since 2000, we've experienced the creation, expansion, and assimilation of the digital world. Before, there was the digital world, which was accessible to a limited demographic, and the physical world, in which we all lived. Through the rapid expansion of wired and wireless data, combined with the explosion of devices capable of connecting us to this network, we live in a new reality that contains both the digital and the physical worlds. Digital, connected technology is as much a part of our daily lives as the microwave and refrigerator, which are now also connected to the Internet.

As the digital world is part of our world, digital citizenship is a component of global citizenship, and is in fact only one of the facets of global digital citizenship that we discuss in this book. It does, however, have the capacity for a tremendous impact on who we are as members of the global community.

Therefore, *global digital citizenship* addresses how we participate and contribute in the blended physical and digital worlds, and how we can leverage the digital world to grow citizens in this new reality. Indeed, we dedicate the work of an entire foundation to this fundamental goal.

Global Digital Citizen Foundation

This book is a natural extension of our Global Digital Citizen Foundation (https://globaldigitalcitizen.org). You see, we have a strong commitment to be leaders in the global transformation of education. Our focus has always been in moving beyond the curriculum content and capitalizing on the opportunity to utilize education to allow children to develop and thrive as whole beings. Indeed, this was always an objective of education, but its focus on standardized testing of content led to content-focused teaching. It left to chance the development of important life skills, such as critical thinking, creativity, and compassion.

As a way to address curriculum while ensuring the development of valuable life skills, we developed what we call the *essential fluencies*, which we outline in our book, *Mindful Assessment* (Crockett & Churches, 2017). We see the emerging importance of developing and evaluating these life skills in the shift toward competency-based curricula that we see in several countries, including New Zealand, Australia, and Canada.

We founded the Global Digital Citizen Foundation with the hope that this work would grow beyond us as authors—that the work of the essential fluencies would grow to empower students to strive together to solve problems that matter and create bright futures for all beings. To that end, we are actively seeking organizations and professionals who share our vision and want to contribute to and expand our vision. We hope that this book will inspire you to work with us to help develop a generation of students into exemplars of global digital citizenship.

Structure of This Book

This book, which we wrote primarily for K–12 educators and administrators, consists of seven chapters on global digital citizenship and three appendices with reproducible resources you can use to support your students. Each chapter ends with a Guiding Questions section to gauge your learning and progress.

We begin chapter 1 with a look at how to evaluate your school's existing acceptable technology use policies and how to update them to reflect the values of global digital citizenship. From forming an advance team to establish the policy's purpose, clarity, and rationale, to creating effective strategies for implementing and supporting it, this chapter lets you hit the ground running.

Chapter 2 discusses the essential traits of the global digital citizen. How can we best develop a student's sense of personal responsibility? How do we teach students to be both good digital and global citizens? What practices bring out their sense of altruism and environmental stewardship? These are all questions we answer.

Chapter 3 focuses on developing sound global digital citizenship agreements that establish key criteria for students taking responsibility for themselves, for each other, and for property. Chapters 4–6 extend on this work by focusing on how you can tailor your technology use agreements to support everyone that must support your students outside the school's walls—the teaching community, the student community, and the wider community.

In chapter 7, we wrap up with a look at embracing teachable moments, including two specific examples of schools whose students reaped the benefits of embracing sound global digital citizenship practices. We also provide a series of learning scenarios you can use in your K–12 classrooms to instill good citizenship thinking and practices in your students.

Finally, we include appendices that provide even more resources you can use. Appendix A includes a series of exercises rooted in learning about and tackling global events and issues that you can use to create mindful moments for your students. Appendix B includes a series of reproducible activity sheets you can use to engage students in understanding the importance of digital citizenship guidelines. Appendix C includes sets of reproducible digital citizenship agreements applicable to students at three learning levels (primary or elementary, middle, and high schools), teaching professionals, and the wider community.

With all this in mind, let's get started!

chapter 1

Evaluating Your Acceptable Use Policy

All schools have at least one acceptable use policy that governs how students use technology within school walls. Frequently, these policies are based on restricting or controlling the use of or access to technology, information, or websites. They often specify a list of sites that are not acceptable (Facebook, for example), behaviors that are not permissible (like using someone else's login details), or technologies that students should not use (personal devices like smartphones, for example). This policy-focused style seldom provides any rationale for school and district decisions and rulings, and it is far from all-encompassing. The policies often address only specific sites, technologies, behaviors, and software—limiting what they cover. They are, at their core, an ineffective means to teaching students how to be good digital citizens, let alone good global digital citizens.

If you want to effect change in your school's digital culture, a critical starting point is understanding where you are. In their book, *Understanding by Design*, Grant Wiggins and Jay McTighe (2005) discuss the importance of knowing where you are, understanding where you want to be, and then using the difference between these—the gap analysis—to develop your plan for reaching your goal. You can apply this concept in assessing your school's or district's acceptable use policy.

In this chapter, we examine the process for establishing a thorough set of ethically driven acceptable use guidelines, which will form the framework for your digital citizenship agreements, by working through the following stages.

- Forming an advance team
- Establishing your purpose
- Ensuring clarity
- Creating a rationale
- Implementing the guidelines
- Supporting the guidelines

We close this chapter with a detailed look at how you manage in-school technology use once your guidelines are in place.

Advance Teams

On May 29, 1953, New Zealander Sir Edmund Hillary and Nepalese Sherpa mountaineer Tenzing Norgay became the first climbers confirmed to reach the summit of Mount Everest ("Edmund Hillary," n.d.). This was not their first visit to the region. Hillary had been part of the British reconnaissance mission in 1951, which served as an advance team for his ultimate climb ("1951 British Mount Everest reconnaissance expedition," n.d.). He understood that before he could make the climb, he had to better understand the environment. Whether you're scaling mountains or transforming school or district culture, to succeed in such an undertaking requires careful, advance planning and deliberate consideration. In fact, before any great event, an advance team should perform a reconnaissance mission to survey the existing landscape.

The initial process of changing a school or district's digital culture is twofold—(1) organize a small committee responsible for obtaining a clear understanding of the goals and (2) investigate the existing policy to determine gaps. For instance, because schools and districts are required to provide reasonable care, the infrastructure blocks many of the policy elements identified as inappropriate or unacceptable when the user connects to the network. However, outside school, when the user connects to his or her personal network, no such restrictions apply. The nature and structure of many acceptable use policies mean they only apply at school and lack the holistic nature that would see users applying the principles in all aspects of their lives.

Effecting this kind of critical cultural change requires a clear vision and input from the various community stakeholders, including staff, parents, students, and school trustees. Establishing an advance team to gain input from the entire community is valuable because it aligns all stakeholder groups. Because large groups often function as a committee from which little emerges, the team should be small with members who are engaged in and motivated by the task. Team members should be early adopters who see the benefits and significance of changes. Often, advance teams develop a champion, who becomes the public face of the change.

Given all of this, what does a better acceptable use policy look like? That's what we look at in the rest of this chapter, beginning with gaining a better understanding of a policy's purpose.

Purpose

When setting out to establish your school's purpose, you must understand what digital citizenship outcomes you want to achieve. These goals should reflect the purpose of education—to prepare young people for life beyond school and enable them to be contributing and valuable citizens.

Consider the approaches taken in various international school systems. In the Australian Curriculum (n.d.a), "Capability encompasses knowledge, skills, behaviours and dispositions. Students develop capability when they apply knowledge and skills confidently, effectively and appropriately in complex and changing circumstances, in their learning at school and in their lives outside school."

In the New Zealand Curriculum, "Key competencies are the capabilities people have, and need to develop, to live and learn today and in the future" (Te Kete Ipurangi, 2014).

In the International Baccalaureate (IB, 2015) curriculum, "The aim of all IB programmes is to develop internationally minded people who, recognizing their common humanity and shared guardianship of the planet, help to create a better and more peaceful world."

Notice that each of these curricula establishes the importance of preparing young minds for life after schooling. They focus not only on learning but also on citizenship. This is not by accident. In designing a curriculum and acceptable technology use guidelines that go hand in hand to enhance both student learning and digital citizenship, it helps to use a tool like the one in figure 1.1 to analyze where you are and where you want to go.

Purpose

What are the outcomes you want to achieve for digital citizenship within your school?

As it is currently, does your acceptable use policy or digital citizenship agreement cover the key areas you previously identified?

◯ Yes   ◯ No

Match outcomes to elements and identify the areas of weakness.

Figure 1.1: Digital citizenship analysis tool.

continued →

Circle the grade levels of the students you are targeting.

K	1	2	3	4	5	6	7	8	9	10	11	12	Postsecondary

Do you have specific documents for different age groups?

○ Yes   ○ No

Is the language of the agreement or documents suitable for the target audience?

• **Readability index:** http://bit.ly/2sjLgPq

• **Lexile scale:** www.lexile.com/analyzer

Implementation

How do you implement the agreement or principles into the school? (Consider training for students, staff, community, process, resources, and so on.)

How often do staff or administrators use the agreement or the principles that the agreement represents in community, school, and classroom activities?

	Never	Once a Year	Once a Term	Once a Week	Daily	Every Lesson
Classroom	○	○	○	○	○	○
Schoolwide	○	○	○	○	○	○
Community	○	○	○	○	○	○

Support Resources

Do you have support resources for the agreement? (These could be learning resources such as posters, or training resources such as presentations and so on.)

○ Yes   ○ No

List the resources you have available.

Monitoring and Consequences

How do you monitor use within your school? What mechanisms do you have in place? (Please consider tools, processes, and frequency.)

What are the consequences that you have in place to deal with inappropriate behavior?

Do the consequences for virtual activities correspond to physical activities?

○ Yes   ○ No

Review and Evaluation

How frequently do you review your acceptable use or digital citizenship agreement and related policies?

	Never	Four to Five Years	Two to Three Years	Annually
Review Cycle	○	○	○	○

How do you review your agreements and policies?

Community Involvement

What level of buy-in and involvement do you have in your digital citizenship program?

	None	Little	Some	Integral
Development				
Students	○	○	○	○
Teachers	○	○	○	○
Wider Community	○	○	○	○

continued →

	None	Little	Some	Integral
Implementation and Training				
Students	○	○	○	○
Teachers	○	○	○	○
Wider Community	○	○	○	○
Monitoring and Use				
Students	○	○	○	○
Teachers	○	○	○	○
Wider Community	○	○	○	○
Review and Reflection				
Students	○	○	○	○
Teachers	○	○	○	○
Wider Community	○	○	○	○

Notes

Visit **go.SolutionTree.com/technology** *for a free reproducible version of this figure.*

By using a tool such as this one, you should begin to develop an understanding of your school's strengths and weaknesses with regard to developing your students into good digital citizens.

Because educators have long-term goals for students beyond school, they must develop students' skills and behaviors not only to prepare them for life but also to enable them to be contributing and functional members of society. Developing a suitable digital citizenship foundation is a key objective and aspirational goal for educators in an increasingly digital world. Well-thought-out and ethically based acceptable use guidelines based on the tenets of digital citizenship can help facilitate that preparation.

Traditional acceptable use agreements aren't really agreements, and we do not refer to them as such in this book. They are based on defined policies that are often limiting, inflexible, and compliance focused. Ethically based digital citizenship agreements instead offer guidelines that the community develops and agrees to that are encompassing and adaptable and focus on the learner's ethical and moral development. Table 1.1 lists some of the traits most common to these agreements.

Table 1.1: Comparing Traditional Acceptable Use Policies and Ethically Based Digital Citizenship Guidelines

Traditional Acceptable Use Policies	Ethically Based Digital Citizenship Guidelines
Applicable only to school environment	Applicable to all aspects of life; holistic
Specific and restrictive	Encompassing
Focused on compliance	Focused on ethics
Inflexible	Adaptable
Struggles to deal with new and emerging technologies, behaviors, and trends	Able to deal with new technologies, behaviors, and trends
Requires frequent updates	Requires seldom updates
Often written in legal or quasi-legal language making them hard to understand, particularly for younger students	Written for the specific age group, using age-appropriate language
Often one agreement for all student ages	Separate agreements that reflect students' ages
Complex and lacking clarity	Clear and understandable

*Visit **go.SolutionTree.com/technology** for a free reproducible version of this table.*

Once you establish the purpose for your digital citizenship guidelines, it's equally important to ensure its language is clear to the intended audience.

Clarity

Many have the experience of installing software and then being asked to agree to the end user license agreement (EULA). Written in a legal language, these documents are long, dull, and often indecipherable to the layman. As a result, most people simply agree to the EULA without ever reading the fine print. Although it suits the license holders to have users do this, it is less than optimal for users. What exactly have you agreed to? What force and effect does it actually have?

Many of the acceptable use policies schools use are similar. In an effort to protect the school or district from potential legal challenges, lawyers often write these policies in such a manner that is unsuitable for the target audience—the students. Students sign them, because without agreeing to the document, they will not have access to the computers and online resources needed to complete their work. Unfortunately, even if the document's terms were negotiable, they either don't understand or don't take the time to read these documents; it's all too hard for them.

Consider this challenge: take your school's acceptable use policy and copy the text into either the SMOG (simplified measure of gobbledygook) Calculator readability index (http://bit.ly/2sjLgPq) or the Lexile Framework for Reading (www.lexile.com/analyzer).

How readable is your agreement? If you are unfamiliar with these tools, we talk more about them in the Student Buy-In section in chapter 5 (page 76).

As you interpret the results from a readability analysis tool, consider the following questions and what they say about your digital citizenship agreement's language.

- Who is your digital citizenship agreement written for? Is the agreement a document the students can use and understand, or is it written to safeguard the school or district from potential litigation?

- How readable is your digital citizenship agreement? Does it suit the target audience's needs?

- Do you have specific agreements for different age groups? Is the language of the agreement suitable for the target audience?

If you can't satisfactorily answer these questions, you need to continue to re-evaluate the language you use in your digital citizenship agreements. Once you've done that, you can start to consider the rationale behind each guideline in the agreement and whether it is justified.

Rationale

Both acceptable use policies and digital citizenship agreements often make statements about what a young person should or should not do online. These well-intended and applicable statements often miss a critical element—the rationale for their existence. In designing guidelines for students, educators, and parents, we believe it's critical to justify each guideline with a compelling case that supports each statement in age-appropriate terms. If you cannot justify and support a guideline, do not include it.

Since one of the goals of digital citizenship agreements is to apply each of their guidelines across all aspects of life, students are unlikely to adopt guidelines that their homes cannot also support. Although students may adhere to restrictive policy agreements at school, where there is a degree of supervision and monitoring, they are likely to ignore them for the other eighteen hours of the day when they are no longer in the learning environment. Ethically driven guidelines, however, stay with students no matter where they are.

After thoroughly examining your digital citizenship agreements, consider the following questions.

- Do they provide clear explanations for each guideline they propose?

- When staff present an agreement to students, do they discuss the guidelines, and do students clearly understand them? Or, are students simply asked to read the agreement and sign it?

In considering these questions, it's important that you identify any weak areas, where an agreement guideline does not provide a suitable rationale for its existence. Consider, for example, the following guidelines for a school grappling with establishing a rationale for social media use.

- **Poor guideline:** The use of social media at school is banned.
- **Better guideline:** The use of social media or any online resources should be educationally focused and not be a distraction to learning.

Understand that the goal is to avoid off-task behavior that negatively impacts student learning outcomes while also accepting that students can productively use social media platforms as tools for online collaboration and peer mentoring. The first guideline does not accomplish this goal, but the second guideline does.

When you have a clearly established rationale for each guideline in a digital citizenship agreement, you can begin to focus on its implementation.

Implementation

Although less common in U.S. schools, in many schools around the world, one of the key aspects of daily life is the school diary. This provides a place for the vital practice of recording the important elements of the school day or week, homework, assessments, and sporting and cultural events. In Andrew's school, at the front of the diary in a place of pride is the digital citizenship agreement. There are three separate, school-specific agreements for each of the district's three different schools—primary (elementary), middle (intermediate and junior high), and high (senior or secondary) school. Parents can also easily access them on the school website.

Each year, the eleventh-grade students work through a series of lessons focused on the digital citizenship agreements and the broader concept of global digital citizenship. The school asks these students to contribute to the process of updating and refreshing each guideline within the digital citizenship agreements. They propose changes and modifications that the school may or may not accept, and that reflect their changing digital environment. A similar process happens in the seventh grade. The school selected these grades because, in the New Zealand curriculum framework, they were the change point from primary school to middle school and from middle school to senior school. These points represent a significant change in the expectations schools place on students and their responsibilities as learners. The students' ages also match well to significant periods of cognitive development and their development of ethical foundations.

Providing students with input and valuing their contribution increase student body buy-in. Any modifications to the school's agreements are made in the spirit and ethos of providing the students with clear and appropriate guidance for global digital citizenship at school and beyond.

However, implementation goes beyond just a few sessions seeking student engagement in the process. It must be more than simply publishing the guidelines in a diary, on posters in the classrooms, or on the school's website. Effective and transformational implementation includes three groups of key stakeholders actively modeling these concepts—(1) students, (2) staff, and (3) the wider community. In particular, teachers' expectations of acknowledgement of sources, fair-use rules, and acceptable online behavior must be so natural and so ingrained that they become part of all teaching.

Consider the following questions.

- How often do staff use the agreements (or the guidelines that the agreements represent) in community, school, and classroom activities? Never? Once per year? Once per term? Once per week? Daily? Every lesson?

- Where are the digital citizenship agreements? Are they displayed in the classroom, made part of the school publications, and immediately at hand? Are they stored away and not easily accessible?

In a perfect world, the agreement guidelines are integrated into all activities that occur across the school. Although it is good to have the agreements as a poster in the room, or appended to the school diary or planner, these are merely starting points. The ultimate goal is still to integrate the principles into everyday teaching and learning so that they become second nature.

With fully developed digital citizenship agreements in place, agreements that include clear and rational guidelines, you can turn your attention to their support.

Support

To make sustainable and long-lasting change for how students use technology, there must be an agreeable and shareable vision from which to derive attainable goals. There must also be a clear process to facilitate the change. The participants must not only want change but also must have the necessary skills to change. Finally, the necessary resources and support to enable change must be in place.

Changing behavior patterns in a digital world requires support resources and processes. It's not enough to simply have a suitable set of guidelines; there must be support resources and processes that make the changes and behaviors sustainable.

These support resources could include using a *spiral curriculum* that embeds age-appropriate teaching opportunities into the teaching and learning framework. The spiral curriculum could offer materials for all members of the school community, including students, parents, teachers, administrators, and board members. Certainly, the spiral curriculum also requires suitable processes for dealing with concerns.

Consider this challenge: list and discuss the agreements' support resources and processes, and then reflect on their efficacy.

Although it is important for each guideline in your digital citizenship agreements to apply inside and outside of school walls, once you craft and implement your digital citizenship agreements, you still need to contend with how your schools govern technology use within the building.

In-School Use

Even with well-crafted and supported use agreements, you will face questions about how you manage technology access within school walls. What level of access do you give students? How do you monitor student use, and what are the consequences for use violations? How does this impact the many stakeholders in your community? The following sections examine each of these in turn.

Access

Although your ultimate goal is for students to monitor their own Internet use, you will still face questions of how to manage students' access to online resources. Many schools either operate under an open-access system (one that operates without content restrictions), or one that uses a blacklist (a list of blocked websites or types of websites) or a whitelist (where students can only access a specific list of preapproved websites). Consider these questions.

- What level of access to online materials and websites does your school have? Consider access to social media, file-sharing sites, collaborative tools (like Google Docs, wikis, and so on), as well as unacceptable materials.

- What mechanisms do you use to manage this access?

- Who makes the decisions about what is accessible and what is not?

- Is this an educational or technical decision?

In our experience, some schools try to restrict access to only the sites that the school deems suitable (a whitelist). As many schools soon discover, the prevalence of smartphones with access to high-speed connectivity, and the ease of setting up a personal hot spot to bypass these restrictions, make these attempts ineffectual. To make matters worse, pushing students to these lengths results in the school losing any ability to track and monitor their activities as they circumvent the restrictive network.

A better solution is one that is rooted in the duty-of-care concept, one that restricts student access to materials that are illegal or, by their nature, inappropriate but permits other types of access. Schools often achieve this by using a category-based filtering system, blocking pornography, hate sites, and gambling and illegal software sites. However, these systems typically enable administrators to make exceptions. For example, online auction sites are often a distraction to students and staff, leading schools to block them. For economics students, however, these sites are beneficial to learning, so administrators can implement an exception for specified group access. In a similar way, some schools enable timed access to social media rather than blocking it across the board—the filtering software enables specific group access before and after school and during breaks and lunch. This creates a privilege for students to respect, one the school can disable for individuals or groups if they abuse it.

When you establish the bounds for what students can and cannot access using school data connections, you must also determine how to monitor student use and apply consequences for violating use terms.

Monitoring and Consequences

You cannot effectively enforce strict online access rules unless you have the infrastructure to monitor what students are doing. You must also know in advance what the consequences are for violations. Consider these questions.

- How do you monitor use within your school? What mechanisms do you have in place? Please consider tools, processes, and frequency.

- What reporting structure do you have in place to deal with unacceptable online materials or actions? Is it the same as other inappropriate behaviors?

- What are the consequences that you have in place to deal with inappropriate online behavior?

Many networking and filtering products can log all users' activities. Depending on the settings, they can record the sites the students or staff members access or visit. They can note the duration of the stay and even user interactions. The log files for an average-size school are enormous. Working through them is tedious, time consuming, and offers a very limited return on time investment for the staff member pouring over them. Fortunately, if the school's filtering software is working efficiently, there should be very little connection to unacceptable sites, making the tedious process of sifting through the log files even less beneficial.

The benefit these logs offer comes when someone on staff raises a concern about technology use. In this case, the evidence hidden in line after line of activity becomes invaluable. In these scenarios, a single staff administrator can quickly search for a specific user's activities during a specified time frame.

In dealing with unacceptable actions and behavior, we often see a marked difference between real-world infractions and those perpetrated in digital mediums. Schools often deal with the theft of a physical object more seriously than an act of online piracy. The fact that we describe it in different terms, theft and piracy, is itself indicative of the different approaches schools take to address these unacceptable actions. Schools should deal with the two actions using similar approaches and consequences.

No matter what monitoring method you use or what consequence you have in place, you must consider that most of these rules can easily go out the window once students leave school grounds. Therefore, an effective use policy requires involvement from the wider community.

Holistic Community Involvement

Reaching global digital citizenship's long-term objectives requires more than what schools can do on their own. As teachers and educators, we see our students for five or six hours per day. This is a considerable amount of time, but there are still another eighteen hours in each day that we are not around and students exist outside schools' monitoring systems. Because schools cannot control what students do in the digital world when they leave school grounds, it is essential that any ethically based use guidelines you establish have buy-in from the wider community. This community includes parents and guardians, boards of trustee members, and the many other adults that influence students' lives. Consider these questions.

- What level of community buy-in and involvement do you have in your current digital citizenship program?

- Were all stakeholders involved in developing, implementing, managing, and monitoring the school's digital citizenship program?

To help answer these questions, conduct the assessment rubrics in figure 1.2. This rubric helps gauge involvement from students, teachers, and the wider community.

Student Community Involvement

	None	Little	Some	A lot
The development of the policy or program	1	2	3	4
The implementation of and training for the policy or program	1	2	3	4
The management of access and filtering for the network	1	2	3	4
The monitoring and use of the network	1	2	3	4
The review and reflection of the policy or program	1	2	3	4

Student community buy-in: ____ / 20

Figure 1.2: Community involvement rubrics.   continued →

Teaching Community Involvement

	None	Little	Some	A lot
The development of the policy or program	1	2	3	4
The implementation of and training for the policy or program	1	2	3	4
The management of access and filtering for the network	1	2	3	4
The monitoring and use of the network	1	2	3	4
The review and reflection of the policy or program	1	2	3	4

Teaching community buy-in: _____ / 20

Wider Community Involvement

	None	Little	Some	A lot
The development of the policy or program	1	2	3	4
The implementation of and training for the policy or program	1	2	3	4
The management of access and filtering for the network	1	2	3	4
The monitoring and use of the network	1	2	3	4
The review and reflection of the policy or program	1	2	3	4

Wider community buy-in: _____ / 20

*Visit **go.SolutionTree.com/technology** for a free reproducible version of this figure.*

Each of these rubrics provides options for choosing an answer corresponding to the estimated involvement level of each community in developing, implementing, and maintaining a digital citizenship agreement framework. Once you've chosen your answers, total them up at the bottom. The closer you are to twenty in each category, the better, but regardless of the score using these rubrics creates a baseline from which you can analyze results and begin a discussion about where you need to focus and improve.

Now that you've read about how to evaluate and validate your own digital citizenship agreements, in the next chapter we'll step beyond policy and look deeper into what the agreements are meant to achieve. You will discover how digital citizenship becomes part of global citizenship, each a defining tenet of your ethically based guidelines that ensure every individual not only adheres to but also unconsciously lives the agreement guidelines of acceptability and fairness. This is where we meet the *global digital citizen.*

Guiding Questions

As you reflect on this chapter, consider the following four guiding questions.

1. What is the *gap analysis*, and how does it apply to evaluating a digital citizenship agreement?

2. Why is it important to use an advance team to gain an understanding of where you are starting from before making any changes?

3. What are the problems and limitations with most schools' acceptable use policies?

4. What are the most important characteristics of an effective digital citizenship agreement?

chapter 2

Uniting Digital Citizenship and Global Citizenship

When the public got its first taste of the World Wide Web, we had little idea of the change it would usher into the world. The Internet we know today continues to grow exponentially. In June 2016, Cisco (2016) estimated that our annual global IP (Internet Protocol) traffic would surpass the zettabyte (ZB) threshold by the end of the year. Cisco (2016) further estimates that we will reach 2.3 ZB per year by the end of 2020.

Our level of global interconnectedness is staggering, with most people incorporating the Internet into many facets of daily life. Its presence is constant, and its absence seems unimaginable. The Internet allows us to become true global citizens, both socially and as a workforce. We can see and track our actions on an international scale. We measure our impact on the global environment and gauge our social and moral differences and similarities. We rally together to inspire hope and provide aid for countries dealing with hardships and tragedies. This interconnectedness allows us to see how local or individual efforts can have a global effect. Seeing the impact of the individual in the global community shows us the great positive potential of the Internet. But, we also see that same impact reveal how exposed we are to scrutiny, manipulation, and threats to our privacy and security.

When you think about it, it makes sense to cultivate empowered individuals who are dutifully aware of their responsibility—both for and with the power of the Internet—for the lasting well-being of our global community. This is a hallmark of the global digital citizen.

We frequently use the phrase *global digital citizen*, but what does that mean? How do we define this individual? A starting point for creating a new level of ethical consciousness among global individuals is to define the characteristics of global digital citizenship, which encompass a range of human qualities that we break down into the tenets listed in figure 2.1 (page 24).

Personal responsibility

Global citizenship

Digital citizenship

Altruistic service

Environmental stewardship

Figure 2.1: Tenets of global digital citizenship.

In this chapter, we examine each of these tenets, why they are important, and what it means to exemplify them. Each of these sections concludes with an assessment rubric derived from chapter 8, "Global Digital Citizenship," of our book, *Mindful Assessment* (Crockett & Churches, 2017). *Mindful Assessment* (Crockett & Churches, 2017) presents complete frameworks for what we call *essential fluencies*—crucial new skills and mindsets learners need to flourish in 21st century life. Global digital citizenship is the last of these six essential fluencies. The global digital citizenship assessment rubrics in this chapter are also available for free online. Go to **go.SolutionTree.com/technology** to access them.

Although we place emphasis in this chapter on the teacher-to-student dynamic, it's important to understand that we must all value and model the tenets of global digital citizenship if we are to instill these values in our youth. We begin with personal responsibility.

Personal Responsibility

For teachers, developing a student's sense of personal responsibility is about gradually shifting the responsibility for learning to the student, and developing his or her sense of accountability for lifelong learning. It includes demonstrating how one governs oneself in matters of finance, ethical and moral boundaries, personal health and fitness, and all relationships. The following sections illustrate the good that comes from internalizing these traits.

- Taking responsibility for lifelong learning
- Nurturing relationships of every definition
- Maintaining physical, mental, and emotional health
- Managing financial matters
- Developing ethical and moral standards

At the end of these sections, we include an assessment framework that explains how to set students on this path and develop them into citizens with a strong sense of personal responsibility.

Taking Responsibility for Lifelong Learning

One of the greatest gifts teachers can give students is developing their capacity and desire to learn independently. The New Zealand Ministry of Education (2007) identifies the following key competencies that support lifelong learning.

- **Thinking:** Using creative, critical, and cognitive processes to make sense of information, experiences, and ideas

- **Using language, symbols, and text:** Understanding and using the codes that express knowledge

- **Managing self:** Developing a can-do attitude and seeing oneself as a capable learner

- **Relating to others:** Interacting effectively with diverse groups in multiple contexts

- **Participating and contributing:** Establishing active involvement in local and wider communities

Through these key competencies, lifelong learning becomes a habit of mind and creates a sense of pride and accomplishment in all of us. Taking responsibility for our learning also adds to our capacity to teach and learn from others.

Nurturing Relationships of Every Definition

Teachers must encourage themselves and their students to learn proper ways to communicate. People enter our lives with unique backgrounds and histories that are often contrary to our own. Understanding and relating to others foster compassion and empathy and help us grow. These traits give us an opportunity to learn from other people, develop our sense of perspective and pluralism, and respond to conflict with civility and constructive thinking. On its website, the Australian Curriculum (n.d.b) identifies the importance and significance of intercultural understanding:

> Intercultural understanding is an essential part of living with others in the diverse world of the twenty-first century. It assists young people to become responsible local and global citizens, equipped through their education for living and working together in an interconnected world.

The curriculum from the New Zealand Ministry of Education (n.d.) also encompasses this critical area by embracing cultural diversity:

Cultural diversity is one of eight principles in *The New Zealand Curriculum* that provide a foundation for schools' decision making. The principle of cultural diversity calls for schools and teachers to affirm students' different cultural identities, and incorporate their cultural contexts into teaching and learning programmes.

Through these practices, we begin to understand all the ways that we are connected to each other despite any cultural differences.

Maintaining Physical, Mental, and Emotional Health

Teacher or student, maintaining a balance between physical, mental, and emotional health within ourselves is essential in helping us better manage our everyday affairs. Some practices for maintaining holistic health can include activities like the following.

- Maintaining regular physical exercise
- Taking up a hobby
- Helping others
- Joining a club or group
- Changing up a daily routine

Having physical vitality, for example, increases our longevity and our ability to enjoy life at any age. Activities that support mental and emotional health help diminish stress on the mind and body and make us more resilient. All of this contributes to whole-being wellness and stability.

Managing Financial Matters

Financial education helps students understand that wealth of any kind comes with responsibilities. Money management encourages the adoption of lifelong smart financial strategies. It shows students the value of hard work and maintaining its rewards.

Developing Ethical and Moral Standards

Treating others with respect lies at the core of every culture's ethical and moral standards. By developing a personal ethical structure, students can learn the fundamental differences between right and wrong, just and unjust, and moral and immoral. It provides students with personal guidelines for living honest and charitable lives, and sets an example for others. This is part of how all of us contribute to the safety and well-being of our whole society.

Establishing a Personal Responsibility Assessment Framework

Figure 2.2 presents a rubric for assessing the development and progression of a global digital citizen's sense of personal responsibility.

Personal Responsibility	Phase 1 (awareness, connection, remembering)	Phase 2 (understanding, applying)	Phase 3 (analyzing, evaluating)	Phase 4 (evaluating, creating)
Integrity	• Sometimes acts with integrity in actions and words and occasionally considers others • Possesses a sense of honesty and sometimes takes responsibility for his or her behavior or actions	• Often acts with integrity in actions and words • Possesses a sense of honesty, justice, and fairness • Usually considers others and interacts with dignity • Sometimes takes responsibility for his or her behavior and actions and accepts the consequences	• Usually acts with integrity in actions and words • Possesses a good sense of honesty, justice, and fairness • Usually considers others and interacts with dignity • Frequently takes responsibility for and reflects on his or her behavior and actions and the consequences	• Acts with integrity in actions and words • Possesses a strong sense of honesty, justice, and fairness • Considers others and interacts with dignity • Takes responsibility for and reflects on his or her behavior, actions, and the consequences
Caring and compassion	• Sometimes shows care and consideration to the people with whom he or she interacts • Sometimes offers support and shows gratitude and appreciation	• Shows some care and consideration to others' needs • Is sometimes supportive and will offer a critique that is appropriate and suitable • Often shows gratitude and appreciation	• Shows caring and consideration for others' needs and the environment • Is generally considerate in his or her actions and understands their impact • Is generally suitably supportive and sometimes proactive • Offers a critique that is generally appropriate and suitable • Shows gratitude and appreciation	• Shows caring and is empathetic to others' needs and the environment • Is considerate and deliberate in his or her actions, weighing their impact before enacting them • Is always supportive, proactive, and considerate • Offers a considerate critique that is appropriate and suitable • Always shows genuine gratitude and appreciation

Figure 2.2: Global digital citizen assessment rubric— personal responsibility.

continued →

Personal Responsibility	Phase 1 (awareness, connection, remembering)	Phase 2 (understanding, applying)	Phase 3 (analyzing, evaluating)	Phase 4 (evaluating, creating)
Accountability	• Shows awareness that his or her actions affect others and that others' actions affect him or her • Occasionally accepts responsibility for his or her actions and attempts to change his or her behaviors	• Shows awareness that he or she has an impact on a personal and local scale • Considers his or her behaviors and actions, often taking responsibility, and applies changes to behaviors and observes results	• Analyzes the impact of his or her behaviors and actions on a personal, local, and global scale • Frequently takes responsibility and often undertakes measures to avoid, reduce, or minimize impacts	• Evaluates the impact of his or her behaviors and actions on a personal, local, and global scale • Accepts responsibility and is proactive in undertaking what measures he or she can to avoid, reduce, or minimize impacts
Curiosity	• Sometimes demonstrates curiosity • Occasionally shows enthusiasm for or a love of learning and discovery • When encouraged, develops skills that help him or her to focus and learn in his or her chosen or preferred areas	• Is often curious and inquiring • Sometimes shows a love of learning and discovery, and shows potential to be a lifelong learner • Continues to develop skills that help focus on and learn new things in chosen or preferred areas	• Frequently is curious and inquiring • Often shows a love of learning and discovery, enjoying opportunities to develop his or her understanding of the world • Shows he or she is a lifelong learner who often develops the skills and motivation required to continue his or her learning journey	• Is curious and inquiring, showing a love of learning and discovery, and actively seeking and enjoying opportunities to develop a deeper and richer understanding of the world • Shows he or she is a lifelong learner who consistently develops and exhibits the skills and motivation required to continue his or her learning journey

Personal Responsibility	Phase 1 (awareness, connection, remembering)	Phase 2 (understanding, applying)	Phase 3 (analyzing, evaluating)	Phase 4 (evaluating, creating)
Courage	• Seldom challenges him- or herself, and can be impetuous and impulsive in his or her challenges and risk taking • Struggles to accept a critique and criticism	• Is sometimes thoughtful and deliberate in his or her actions, but other times is impetuous • May deliberately challenge him- or herself by undertaking tasks or participating in activities that are beyond his or her current skill level or comfort zone, but prefers to remain within his or her comfort zone • Accepts criticism with good grace and sometimes reflects on it	• Is often thoughtful and deliberate in his or her actions • Sometimes deliberately challenges him- or herself, undertaking tasks or participating in activities that are beyond his or her current skill level or comfort zone • Generally accepts criticism with good grace and reflects on it	• Is always thoughtful and deliberate in his or her actions • Challenges him- or herself, undertaking tasks or participating in activities that are beyond his or her current skill level or comfort zone, understanding that such endeavors will help him or her grow and develop • Accepts criticism with good grace and reflects on it
Independence	• Shows little independence and requires extensive support to complete tasks	• Shows some independence and can complete most tasks with some support or guidance • Shows ability to apply feedback to successfully complete tasks	• Shows ability to break the task into elements and then work through them with a degree of independence and self-management • Requires little input or support to successfully complete tasks • Is often self-critical and monitors his or her own progress, and often modifies his or her planning and schedule as a result	• Shows ability to work effectively, efficiently, independently, or without close supervision or guidance • Requires little or no input or support to successfully complete tasks • Is consistently self-critical, monitors his or her own progress and reflects on it, and modifies his or her planning and schedule as a result

continued →

Personal Responsibility	Phase 1 (awareness, connection, remembering)	Phase 2 (understanding, applying)	Phase 3 (analyzing, evaluating)	Phase 4 (evaluating, creating)
Balance	• Has an awareness of his or her current state of balance, but struggles to take suitable steps to maintain a balanced lifestyle	• Attempts to be balanced in his or her physical, emotional, and intellectual well-being • Often applies changes to attempt to manage imbalances, though they are often reactive rather than proactive	• Is often balanced in his or her physical, emotional, and intellectual health • Analyzes his or her personal situation and takes suitable steps to maintain or rebalance his or her needs and requirements • Is often considerate of the emotional, physical, and intellectual well-being of others	• Maintains constant balance in his or her physical, emotional, and intellectual health • Evaluates his or her personal situation and is often proactive in taking steps to maintain or rebalance his or her needs and requirements • Considers his or her emotional, physical, and intellectual well-being and is considerate of others' requirements and needs in these aspects of life
Perseverance	• Occasionally shows determination • Struggles to remain focused on tasks and goals, often quitting when the task becomes challenging	• Often shows a degree of determination and persistence • Often remains focused on tasks and goals • Sometimes moves beyond his or her comfort zone with encouragement to achieve a challenge or complete a task	• Often shows determination and persistence • Shows ability to focus on achieving suitable challenges, goals, and objectives • Is reflective and refines his or her goals • Is frequently realistic or optimistic, and often moves beyond his or her comfort zone to achieve a challenge or complete a task	• Shows constant determination and persistence, and focuses on achieving suitable, considered challenges, goals, and objectives • Is always reflective and is able to, when required, refine goals and judge his or her progress toward milestones • Demonstrates both realism and optimism • Readily moves beyond his or her comfort zone to achieve a challenge or complete a task

❤ Personal Responsibility	Phase 1 (awareness, connection, remembering)	Phase 2 (understanding, applying)	Phase 3 (analyzing, evaluating)	Phase 4 (evaluating, creating)
Resilience	• Struggles to accept criticism, often taking it as a personal slight • When faced with a challenge, sometimes avoids it rather than persisting • In a challenging situation, either completely avoids any form of support and assistance, or else relies completely on the support of others • Struggles to maintain a mature outlook	• Often accepts criticism, sometimes applying suitable actions resulting from this • Sometimes is persistent, occasionally overcoming adversity and intolerance • When faced with challenges, often seeks support • Shows a desire to work toward developing a mature, thoughtful, and determined outlook	• Shows progress toward developing resilience • Shows ability to reflect on criticism, often taking on the relevant elements • Frequently persists to overcome adversity and intolerance • Faces challenges and often seeks support • Frequently demonstrates a mature, thoughtful, and determined outlook on life	• Demonstrates constant resilience • Shows ability to reflect on criticism, evaluating its worth and taking on the relevant elements • Persists to overcome adversity and intolerance • Realistically faces both internal and external challenges and seeks support when required • Demonstrates a mature, thoughtful, and determined outlook on life
Efficiency	• Is sometimes accurate in his or her execution of the plan or product development	• Applies the plan or design with some accuracy; there is some waste in terms of time, effort, and materials or resources	• Generally works efficiently, and there is minimal waste in terms of time, effort, and materials or resources • Demonstrates general accuracy in the execution of his or her plans, product development, and reflection	• Works with efficiency in a manner that is economical in terms of time, effort, and materials or resources • Works with accuracy in the execution of his or her plans, product development, and reflection

continued →

Personal Responsibility	Phase 1 (awareness, connection, remembering)	Phase 2 (understanding, applying)	Phase 3 (analyzing, evaluating)	Phase 4 (evaluating, creating)
Reflection	• Has some awareness of his or her strengths and weaknesses and can occasionally take actions to support him- or herself	• Is sometimes thoughtful and reflective • Shows a broad understanding of his or her strengths and weaknesses and can sometimes take actions to support him- or herself or the community	• Is often thoughtful and reflective • Analyzes his or her strengths and weaknesses and takes some thoughtful actions to support him- or herself, the community, and beyond	• Is constantly thoughtful and reflective • Thoughtfully evaluates his or her actions, learning, and behaviors and considers the strengths and weaknesses of these • Takes actions to support him- or herself, the community, and beyond

Visit **go.SolutionTree.com/technology** for a free reproducible version of this figure.

It is important to understand the purpose of this rubric and those that follow in this chapter. It is not intended as a summative judgment of a person, but rather a formative discussion of what is possible. We have not presented benchmarks for age levels as every individual, depending on life circumstances, will be at different levels. Stress, for example, could play a major role in our ability to evaluate, and we may instead simply react. Additionally, the evaluative capacity we expect to see from an individual varies from person to person. Using these measures as a formative tool allows us to reflect on who we are, what we value, and what we want to be.

Global Citizenship

In a world where an Australian follower can retweet an American user's tweet and have a Pakistani citizen see it moments later, we are all global citizens. *Global citizenship* involves recognizing and fostering how 21st century technology transcends the physical boundaries between citizens of the world by enabling communication, collaboration, dialogue, and debate across all levels of society. The following sections detail the importance of recognizing and fostering a student's presence in the global community and the personal connections within that community. We also talk about understanding the concept of circles of possibilities that affect how all of us can make our mark on the world. We conclude this topic with a framework for assessing student progress toward becoming good global citizens.

Recognizing and Fostering Global Community

Because we are part of a global community, barriers of time and distance no longer exist. This brings about an awareness that technology instantaneously connects us with the world, and with that comes personal and communal responsibilities. We have the means to help and support people all over the world, in addition to those in our local communities. This may seem a Herculean task, but the goal is not to solve all the problems of every community around the world. The goal is to recognize and empathize with others' struggles while endeavoring to contribute to positive solutions wherever possible. We believe that guiding students to this realization helps foster more respect for the various traditions, values, faiths, beliefs, opinions, and practices of a global community.

Recognizing and Fostering Personal Connections

The connectivity that brings us together as global citizens brings with it new personal connections. For example, you may be surprised to learn that 35 percent of couples married between 2005 and 2012 first met online and report they are more satisfied than other couples (Magid, 2013). Having connections of every kind shows us the benefits of being able to share our ideas with more people than ever before. It encourages acceptance, sensitivity, and humility in dealing with others.

Students must learn to see the marketplace they will become a part of as global citizens and recognize the significance of their ability to use shared technology to do work all over the world. They must learn to manage many relationships with peers and colleagues all over the globe and understand why, thanks to technology and the connectivity it provides, it has never been easier to foster and renew relationships with faraway people. For example, a classroom can connect with global learners and established professionals using applications like Skype. Likewise, websites like Kiva (www.kiva.org) allow learners to use microlending to help entrepreneurs in poorer world regions get started on their own business ventures.

Understanding Circles of Possibilities

Further cementing links between personal connections and global communities is also about recognizing what we call circles of possibilities. Ask yourself this question, How do you see the world? When Lee's Japanese sensei first asked him this question, he had an immediate response, one that came without considering the meaning of the question or his deepest feelings. Maybe you also had such a response when you read this question.

Some see the world through the lens of fear, that the world is not safe. These individuals are constantly concerned about what the world will take from them. Others see the world through curiosity, and to them the world is a wondrous place full of possibilities and opportunities. Many see the problems that the world faces and feel a sense of despair. This despair can be so painful that these individuals find distractions to escape reflecting on human suffering and their own feelings of helplessness. Our students, who are our children, feel this too.

What we believe has been most beneficial in building capacity in students, teachers, and administrators alike is an understanding of what all of us can do and how that leads to change. If you knew for certain you would succeed, that you would solve the problem which is your greatest concern, would you take action? Of course you would. This empowerment is reflective of a growth mindset as opposed to a fixed mindset— that is to say, that achievement is a factor of effort and not fixed ability (Dweck, 2006).

This is the point at which we introduce students to circles of possibilities. We ask students to consider what is possible at various levels and then take action based on what *can* be done. The levels start with *me*, and then expand to encompass *family*, *community*, *country*, and the *world*.

- **Me:** What can you do to solve this problem within your own life? If you never spoke about it, blamed or judged others, but only altered your own thoughts and actions, what could you do?

- **Family:** How do you affect the choices your family makes? Consider that once you have accomplished all you can do, you have already begun to impact your family, just through the example you set. Because your capacity to impact your family is limited by your own efforts, the greater your actions and convictions then the greater the impact on your family.

- **Community:** How can you and your family impact your community? Consider not just where you live, but all your communities such as school, clubs, and organizations that you belong to.

- **Country:** How can you, along with your family and communities, create change in your country?

- **World:** How can you, your family, communities, and country transform the world?

In asking students to think about these circles of possibilities, have them consider the following facts about bottled water (D'Alessandro, 2014; Pacific Institute, 2007).

- Producing the yearly bottles for American consumption requires the equivalent of more than seventeen million barrels of oil, not including the energy for transportation.

- Bottling water produces more than 2.5 million tons of carbon dioxide.

- It takes three liters of water to produce one liter of bottled water.

- A one-liter bottle in the ocean can break down into fragments so small that a piece could be found on every mile of beach in the world.

- We only recycle 5 percent of the plastics we produce, and virtually every piece of plastic ever made still exists in one form or another.

Ask students to consider that if the environmental havoc the bottled water industry causes is overwhelming to them, they could simply never purchase or drink from a plastic bottle again. They could carry a refillable bottle and use it instead. Likewise, they could even keep a set of cutlery in a bag rather than use the plastic cutlery found in the school cafeteria or fast food restaurants. We're sure you and your students can think of other examples, but you get the point.

All this begs the question: Does this solve the global problem of plastics? You or your students may think that it doesn't, but we disagree. In this scenario, an individual is doing 100 percent of what he or she can do to solve the problem. When enough people do the same, spreading from individuals, to families, to communities, and so on, the problem is solved. It is a similar question to asking, "Does your vote count?" Who would be elected if nobody voted? When students understand that they can solve a problem by taking action within their capacity, they only see possibilities of what more they can do.

Because the levels beyond *me* are where we tend to lay blame, many think their actions don't matter because it's not in their control. It's the government's fault, the school's fault, the test's fault, the media's fault, and so on. Ask your students to consider this: When we lay blame at the feet of others, we also surrender to them our power to solve it. After all, if it's their fault, then they are the only ones that can fix it and so we are powerless and at their mercy.

No matter at what level you work—me, family, community, country, world—you impact all other levels. Your efforts matter because without you it is not possible for everyone to change. What will you do? The answer always starts with *me*.

Establishing a Global Citizenship Assessment Framework

Figure 2.3 (page 36) presents a rubric for assessing the development and progression of a global digital citizen's sense of global citizenship.

Global Citizenship	Phase 1 (awareness, connection, remembering)	Phase 2 (understanding, applying)	Phase 3 (analyzing, evaluating)	Phase 4 (evaluating, creating)
Global awareness	• Has an awareness of some broader global issues • Is sometimes considerate and may report inappropriate behavior	• Displays characteristics of an emerging global citizen • Shows some understanding of existing cultural, religious, and gender differences • Often shows respect for other peoples' customs and beliefs • Demonstrates that he or she is developing an understanding of the value and worth of diversity • Generally is intolerant of inappropriate behavior and occasionally takes steps to report it	• Displays characteristics of a developing global citizen • Analyzes cultural, religious, and gender differences and uses them to guide his or her actions • Shows respect for other peoples' customs and beliefs • Will sometimes value and celebrate differences as part of a rich human tapestry • Generally is intolerant of racist, abusive, sexist, or inappropriate behavior and sometimes takes steps to report it	• Displays the characteristics of a global citizen • Considers and evaluates cultural, religious, and gender differences and mediates his or her actions and interactions by considering them • Consistently shows respect and care for other peoples' customs and beliefs • Values and celebrates differences as part of a rich human tapestry • Shows intolerance of racist, abusive, sexist, or inappropriate behavior and, where possible, takes the appropriate steps to prevent or report it

Global Citizenship	Phase 1 (awareness, connection, remembering)	Phase 2 (understanding, applying)	Phase 3 (analyzing, evaluating)	Phase 4 (evaluating, creating)
Political awareness	• Has little understanding of governance or current issues • Is often guided to support a particular stance, party, or standpoint	• Has rudimentary understanding of governance from a local, national, and global perspective • Has some understanding of historical, current, and emerging issues • Follows the legal requirements for participation in local and national events	• Shows a developing sense of political awareness • Has some understanding of governance from a local, national, and global perspective • Analyzes historical, current, and emerging issues and breaks them down into their components • Can provide some limited evaluation of bias • Forms his or her own political stance on issues and may support parties, groups, or organizations that support his or her viewpoint	• Shows political awareness and is a contributing member of society • Has a broad understanding of governance from a local, national, and global perspective • Analyzes and evaluates historical, current, and emerging issues, separating the issue from political rhetoric, bias, and media spin • Forms his or her own political stance on issues that are critical to him or her and supports parties, groups, or organizations that uphold an appropriate ethical and moral standpoint

Figure 2.3: Global digital citizen assessment rubric—global citizenship.

Visit **go.SolutionTree.com/technology** *for a free reproducible version of this figure.*

Digital Citizenship

To have digital citizenship is to engage in appropriate and exemplary behavior in an online environment. The essence of digital citizenship is about shifting accountability for appropriate behavior from teachers to students, which fosters independence and personal responsibility. This shifting of responsibility includes ensuring that students show respect for self, others, and property. We conclude this topic with a framework for assessing a student's progress and growth as a digital citizen.

Showing Respect and Responsibility for Self

Having respect for yourself is about being aware of how you portray yourself with your online persona. Students must start thinking critically about the short- and long-term effects of the information and images they post, and the value of being private when necessary. Students must be able to set a positive example for others to follow.

Students must be mindful to stay away from behavior that puts them at risk, both online and offline. Acting responsibly encourages exemplary personal governance as a habit of mind and adds to a student's sense of self-worth and self-esteem (Blitzer, Petersen, & Rodgers, 1993). It also reminds him or her of the little things like safely and effectively password-protecting information, and, when appropriate, securing property and resources.

Showing Respect and Responsibility for Others

It's important for students to always consider the consequences of behavior, such as bullying, flaming, harassing, and online stalking—the evidence is everywhere (Chambers, 2013). When an individual attacks someone else online, his or her target is obliged to respond in kind. This perpetuates a cycle of escalation that can and has resulted in consequences in the physical world. Respecting others teaches students the value of being constructive and friendly online. It encourages them to model behavior for others, like responding to online conflicts with a sense of civility and constructive thinking.

Both teachers and students must learn to discourage and report abusive and inappropriate behavior and recognize that there is potential for great harm in forwarding or sharing potentially inappropriate or harmful information or images. This is how we come to see the value in making others feel protected, and therefore valued themselves. In our experience, people who feel valued are less likely to engage in destructive behavior.

Showing Respect and Responsibility for Property

Teachers must consistently stress the importance of asking permission to share another's intellectual property. How we give credit to creators of intellectual property (by properly citing sources and authorship) says much about our respect for those who devote their time to creativity in the service of others. Exploring fair-use rules and copyright laws, and how they apply to sourcing and using online information, is a crucial part of respecting another's property.

We believe that teaching students to treat their own and others' property with care and respect, including intellectual property, is vital to preserving a sense of digital and global community. Instead of stealing images, teach students to use free or open-source resources and learn how to properly search for and recognize them. Both Google and Flickr include features that support searching for Creative Commons or royalty free images (Crockett, 2016). This reminds them that any kind of digital piracy is still theft, and that this theft is not a victimless crime. As such, they make a choice to act with integrity and to value what they use or own.

Establishing a Digital Citizenship Assessment Framework

Figure 2.4 presents a rubric for assessing the development and progression of a global digital citizen's sense of digital citizenship.

Digital Citizenship	Phase 1 (awareness, connection, remembering)	Phase 2 (understanding, applying)	Phase 3 (analyzing, evaluating)	Phase 4 (evaluating, creating)
Respect and responsibility for self	• Has an awareness of some of the online risks and appropriate strategies for personal online safety • Sometimes takes steps to protect him- or herself	• Frequently applies appropriate strategies in his or her online behavior and to minimize exposure to risk • Takes some steps to protect his or her integrity, privacy, data, or identity • Sometimes seeks support or reports abuse	• Is often considerate with his or her online behavior • Takes steps to protect his or her integrity, privacy, data, and identity • Analyzes and evaluates his or her situation and takes steps to minimize his or her exposure to risk • Often seeks support and reports abuse to relevant authorities	• Shows regular deliberation and consideration of his or her online behavior • Takes all suitable steps to protect his or her integrity, privacy, data, and identity • Evaluates his or her situation and is both proactive and reactive toward minimizing his or her exposure to risk • Seeks support and reports abuse to relevant authorities

Figure 2.4: Global digital citizen assessment rubric— digital citizenship.

continued →

Digital Citizenship	Phase 1 (awareness, connection, remembering)	Phase 2 (understanding, applying)	Phase 3 (analyzing, evaluating)	Phase 4 (evaluating, creating)
Respect and responsibility for others	• Has an awareness of the guidelines, norms, and protocols for interactions with other people in a digital environment • Can sometimes be respectful and considerate in his or her interactions	• Follows the guidelines, norms, and protocols for interactions with other people in a digital environment • Is generally respectful and considerate in his or her interactions	• Is often considerate in his or her online behavior • Often considers the needs and privacy of others • Is predominantly respectful in his or her interactions and considerate of other cultures and perspectives • Often shows intolerance for abuse • Considers situations and often takes steps to protect the safety and security of others	• Shows consistent deliberation and consideration in his or her online behavior • Considers the needs and privacy of others • Is respectful in his or her interactions, considerate of other cultures and perspectives, and intolerant of abuse • Evaluates and considers situations on an ethical and moral basis and takes appropriate steps to protect the safety, privacy, security, and identity of others
Respect and responsibility for property	• Has an awareness of the laws of copyright, intellectual property, and privacy • Occasionally cites sources in a suitable manner	• Can follow the guidelines and norms for digital property • Shows an understanding of the laws surrounding copyright, intellectual property, and privacy and sometimes applies them • Occasionally requests permission to use resources and suitably cites sources	• Is often thoughtful in his or her online actions • Shows a general understanding of the laws surrounding copyright, intellectual property, and privacy and often applies them • Sometimes requests permission to use property, acknowledges ownership, and cites resources	• Shows consistent deliberation and consideration in his or her online actions • Possesses a deep and rich understanding of the laws surrounding copyright, intellectual property, and privacy and applies them ethically • Requests permission to use property and abides by the owners' rights to deny use • Is always respectful and responsible in acknowledging ownership, citing resources, and protecting and securing sites and data • Is considerate of and reciprocal to others' requests to use his or her intellectual property

*Visit **go.SolutionTree.com/technology** for a free reproducible version of this figure.*

Altruistic Service

To embody altruistic service is to have a healthy concern for the well-being of people who share our world. It includes creating meaningful physical-world connections with others, embracing the opportunity to practice philanthropy and charity with others, and establishing compassion by association, all without thought of personal gain. We conclude this topic with a framework for assessing a student's sense of altruism.

Creating Meaningful Connections With Others

The ways we are connected to each other go far beyond the realm of social media. Our connections soar ever higher through shared emotions and experiences. With such connections, students learn the importance of having healthy relationships in their lives, and this adds to their capacity for teaching and learning from others. In our experience, it also hones their personal communication and interaction skills.

Practicing Philanthropy and Charity

Practicing compassion and empathy helps us grow personally (Zhang & Chen, 2016). Through charitable acts, students realize that those less fortunate are not less deserving than they are, and that there is value in reasonably and fairly sharing with others. Acting with civility and proactively thinking about others guide students toward building a better space, community, and world environment for everyone.

Establishing Compassion by Association

We believe that constructively sharing others' mental and emotional burdens often makes them lighter and more manageable. Think of an instance when you have helped someone through a challenging time by sharing a relatable experience, or even just by listening without judgment as they expressed their frustration or sadness. When students learn that many of their experiences are similar to those of others, it lets them be more understanding and compassionate. It allows them to serve others better by remembering how people helped them in their past.

Establishing Altruistic Service Assessment Framework

Figure 2.5 (page 42) presents a rubric for assessing a student's progress toward becoming altruistic.

Altruistic Service	Phase 1 (awareness, connection, remembering)	Phase 2 (understanding, applying)	Phase 3 (analyzing, evaluating)	Phase 4 (evaluating, creating)
Problem finding	• Struggles to identify problems independently and frequently requires support and guidance	• Describes and explains situations or issues on a local, regional, or global scale • Can broadly consider the level of need and some of the potential impacts that his or her support could make	• Analyzes situations or issues on a local, regional, or global scale and breaks them down into their components • Can identify and consider areas of need, the level of need, and some of the potential impacts that his or her support could make • Investigates and researches the concern	• Analyzes and evaluates situations or issues on a local, regional, or global scale to identify areas of need • Considers and evaluates the level of need and the impact that his or her support can make in resolving this • Investigates and researches the concern to discern if the need is genuine, legitimate, and worthy of support
Problem solving	• Is often involved in service superficially, minimally, or as a matter of compliance to school or organizational requirements	• Understands the need for altruistic service, and actively participates in service • Often reviews his or her actions	• Analyzes the need for altruistic service • Provides limited or superficial evaluation of the need • Develops and structures a plan or process that partly helps to resolve the issue or need • Actively undertakes altruistic service, including supporting and organizing, and reviews his or her actions	• Evaluates the need for altruistic service and validates that need, ensuring that his or her actions or support are beneficial to the intended recipient • Develops and structures a plan or process that helps resolve or mitigate the issue or need • Arranges, organizes, promotes, supports, or enacts altruistic service in its varied forms through action • Actively reviews and critiques his or her process and refines, adjusts, or terminates his or her actions as required

Figure 2.5: Global digital citizen assessment rubric— altruistic service.

*Visit **go.SolutionTree.com/technology** for a free reproducible version of this figure.*

Environmental Stewardship

Environmental stewardship is a demonstration of commonsense values and an appreciation for the beauty and majesty that surround us every day. It encourages students to explore how to manage Earth's resources, care for the environment, and show responsibility for a global community by acting on personal, local, regional, national, and international levels. We conclude this topic with a framework for assessing a student's ability to be a good steward of his or her environment.

Managing Resources

Managing resources helps us understand how people in poorer countries can live happily with much less. For example, when it comes to the average person living in the Western Hemisphere, how much food or water go to waste? How much unnecessary power do industrialized nations use when leaving lights on in unoccupied rooms? For students, making considerations like these encourages them to strive toward wisely using what they have and not being wasteful. As they look toward global community involvement in the economic use of resources we all share, they contribute to the prosperity and longevity of future generations.

Caring for the Environment

Looking after the environment shows we take pride in the places we call our homes be they global, communal, or domestic. Such practices begin with simple actions on a personal level—keeping our homes clean and energy-efficient, avoiding littering, respecting the community practices of other cultures when traveling, and so on. Students must understand that a healthy environment directly affects their personal health and wellness, and that a healthy ecosystem is essential for all life to continue to prosper. Generations that come after us will hopefully mirror our habitually positive actions toward the environment, ensuring a cycle of global sustainability.

Showing Responsibility for a Global Community

Working to create a healthy world brings cultures together for a mutually beneficial pursuit. It allows students to discover just how much they need strong communities for survival. Contributing to a healthy world environment can improve such economic industries as tourism and importing and exporting. In the end, it also makes us more mindful of conserving precious natural resources. For example, Lee works with Bethlehem University in Palestine to connect students in schools around the world with students there. Together they explore and share solutions to environmental concerns in their respective communities. It is early in the project, but already he is seeing a deeper understanding of and respect for different cultures as learners realize that we are all alike and face similar challenges.

Establishing Environmental Stewardship Assessment Framework

Figure 2.6 presents a rubric for assessing a student's development as a steward of the environment.

Environmental Stewardship	Phase 1 (awareness, connection, remembering)	Phase 2 (understanding, applying)	Phase 3 (analyzing, evaluating)	Phase 4 (evaluating, creating)
Personal awareness and action	• Has some awareness of environmental issues that impact him or her • Sometimes participates in actions to reduce environmental impact or damage	• Often shows interest in his or her environment • Has some understanding of the impact of his or her actions and those of the community and nation on the environment • Sometimes takes personal responsibility for his or her actions and undertakes actions to reduce the environmental cost	• Shows interest in his or her environment • Can analyze short- and long-term impacts of his or her actions and those of the community and nation on the environment and break them down into their components • Often takes personal responsibility for his or her actions and undertakes suitable and sustainable actions to reduce the environmental cost	• Shows an active interest in his or her environment, analyzing and evaluating the short- and long-term impact of his or her actions and lifestyle and those of the community and nation on the environment • Takes personal responsibility for his or her actions and moderates his or her behaviors and actions to reduce the environmental cost • Investigates, evaluates, and undertakes whatever preventative, restorative, and sustainable measures are feasible

Environmental Stewardship	Phase 1 (awareness, connection, remembering)	Phase 2 (understanding, applying)	Phase 3 (analyzing, evaluating)	Phase 4 (evaluating, creating)
Global awareness and action	• Has an awareness of some of the environmental issues and, when encouraged, may participate in activities to reduce or raise awareness of them	• Has an interest in and understanding of some environmental issues • Supports local environmental activities, sometimes taking a stand on significant issues	• Shows an interest in global environmental issues and investigates causes or concerns before offering support • Often takes a stand on current matters, undertaking appropriate actions that raise awareness • Sometimes shows stewardship of his or her world	• Shows an active interest in global environmental issues • Validates causes or concerns before offering support • Takes a stand on matters of importance, undertaking appropriate actions that raise awareness of concerns through legitimate and appropriate means • Shows stewardship, care, and responsibility for his or her world • Thinks globally while acting locally
Environmental stewardship as a consumer	• Has awareness of environmental issues associated with the production, distribution, and disposal of products • Can sometimes consider these factors when making a purchase	• Understands the importance of purchasing power • Understands some of the environmental or societal costs of purchases, supply chains, and manufacturing processes • Is often guided by product labeling as a form of ethical or moral guidance • Applies general guidelines for appropriate purchases	• Understands the impact of purchasing power as a force for change • Analyzes the environmental or societal costs of his or her purchases, the supply chain, and manufacturing base • Analyzes product labeling and often makes informed decisions regarding purchases based on his or her overall analysis • Makes purchasing decisions with consideration for ethical and moral issues	• Considers the impact of purchasing power as a force for change • Evaluates the environmental and societal costs of his or her purchases, the supply chain, and manufacturing base before deciding to buy • Analyzes and evaluates product labeling and makes informed decisions regarding purchases • Makes purchasing decisions based on an informed ethical and moral stance

Figure 2.6: Global digital citizen assessment rubric— environmental stewardship.

*Visit **go.SolutionTree.com/technology** for a free reproducible version of this figure.*

Connecting these tenets of digital and global citizenship forms the foundation for growing students into full-fledged global digital citizens, but it is only a start. To effect this growth in students, you must understand just how much different their experience is from those of prior generations so that you can translate these tenets of global digital citizenship into practical applications of respect and responsibility.

Respect and Responsibility

A respectful and responsible global digital citizen's awareness includes seeing a need to understand a rapidly changing digital landscape and prescribe safety parameters for our most vulnerable users. Our duties of citizenship, however, are more than just obligations in the virtual world. They extend beyond the digital world into all facets of human life and relationships.

Older generations experienced the arrival of a great technological presence with the Internet. For digital students, it's much different because the Internet already existed and ingratiated itself into our way of life before they were born. Whereas we spent a lot of time going online, they were born online. This is the digital revolution that transforms everything for us and them, especially teaching and learning.

The paradigm that older generations have adopted as their guiding mantra is, "You wouldn't do this in the physical world, so why would you do this online?" What you must understand is for the digital student, there is a seamless integration between these two worlds. In many ways, the physical and virtual worlds are inseparable and even one and the same. It's the primary reason for the need to cultivate online behaviors of respect and responsibility for oneself, others, and property, and to ensure that those online disciplines translate back to everything students do in the physical world. This is the beginning of the connection between digital citizenship and global citizenship, and how the two become one.

Through the practice of modeling respect and taking responsibility for oneself, others, and property in the digital world, teachers are in fact growing in their students the tenets of global digital citizenship. Table 2.1 makes clear how global digital citizenship and these applications of respect and responsibility relate.

In the schools we work with, we focus only on digital citizenship, and students start to make the connections to how it globally applies. Thus, their reality becomes, "I wouldn't do this online; why would I do it in the physical world?" By focusing simply on digital citizenship, we are really focusing on cultivating a holistic, responsible, and ethical global citizen in a digital world.

In the next chapter, we look at the digital citizenship agreements that we designed at the Global Digital Citizen Foundation. Thousands of schools across the world use these agreements to foster the mindsets of the caring and compassionate digital citizens

Table 2.1: Connecting the Tenets of Global Digital Citizenship With Applications of Respect and Responsibility

Global Digital Citizen Tenet	Application
Personal responsibility	Respect and responsibility for self
Global citizenship	Respect and responsibility for others
Digital citizenship	Respect and responsibility for self, others, and property
Altruistic service	Respect and responsibility for others
Environmental stewardship	Respect and responsibility for property

in our students. We explore the details of three separate agreements—one each for primary, middle, and high school—and talk a little about why each guideline is so important in the quest to help students become true global digital citizens.

Guiding Questions

As you reflect on this chapter, consider the following five guiding questions.

1. What are the five tenets of global digital citizenship and their defining characteristics? Evaluate each of them.

2. How do each of the tenets support each other in visualizing a holistic global digital citizen?

3. How do the digital citizen and the global citizen relate to each other?

4. What are some examples of how online behaviors impact your experiences in the physical world?

5. What do you notice your own students doing to practice global digital citizenship?

chapter 3

Crafting Digital Citizenship Guidelines

In chapter 1, we established the importance of using an advance team to bring into focus what's most important in a digital citizenship agreement for your school. By establishing a clear purpose and rationale for the agreement's guidelines, you make it possible for your school to successfully implement and support it. In chapter 2, we established the five tenets of global digital citizenship and detailed why they are important. In this chapter, we use these ideas to construct a coherent set of digital citizenship agreements that are built on ethically driven guidelines that reflect the values of a global digital citizen.

Reaching the point where you have established a constructive set of digital citizenship agreements often requires reflecting on the policies you currently have in place. This was a crucial step at Andrew's own school, and we reflect on that process in this chapter. After this brief look back at that experience, we examine a series of digital citizenship agreements for students at the primary (elementary), middle, and high school levels and establish the importance of the guidelines they contain.

A Look Back

Andrew's school, the Kristin School in Auckland, New Zealand, was an early adopter of one-to-one technologies. It implemented its program six months after Methodist Ladies' College in Melbourne did so in 1990, which was the first school in the world to make laptops available to students on a one-to-one basis. Both schools held the master lease for the laptops, and the students leased these laptops from the schools. The software ran a Windows-based platform, and both schools restricted administration rights to the IT (information technology) staff. Internet access was either through a wired connection or the cutting-edge wireless technology of the time.

Like many schools, the Kristin School started with an acceptable use policy that detailed specifically what students could or could not do and what sites they were or were not allowed to visit. The agreement was typical of the time. Students and parents had to sign it before the school gave them access to either their computer or the network. Since ownership of the computer rested with the school, it could recall computers at any time and check for any deviations from the school's prescribed rules. Students did take their laptops home at night, but often students experienced log-in issues working on their home networks because the administrative password was a closely guarded secret. The school needed a better solution.

Despite these troubles, it persisted with this approach and agreement until the advent of bring your own device (BYOD) changed the virtual playground. Schools no longer owned the devices, and so the rights of search and seizure also changed. Schools could no longer restrict websites and information students had access to at home. This was not the only change; the virtual environment was changing and evolving at a rate that made changing what students could or couldn't do with their devices irrelevant. There was simply no way for IT administrators to keep up. The plethora of connected devices as varied as watches, phones, tablets, phablets, netbooks, and notebooks quickly outstripped the ability of even the most capable IT team to manage.

It was the birth of BYOD and the demise of the managed laptop program that forced the Kristin School to shift from restrictive and limited sets of rules to an encompassing and ethically based approach that better serves students and administration alike. This new approach stretches beyond the classroom to practically govern students' across-the-board technology use. It is adaptable and flexible enough to cover most eventualities. It is an approach that covers personal, interpersonal, and intellectual property-based aspects of the students' and staff members' interactions with digital devices. These guidelines also fit equally well with physical world behavioral expectations.

This scenario isn't just applicable to the Kristin School. This new digital citizenship model, matched with a BYOD program, suits schools worldwide because it changes the approach from defining acceptable use policies toward one that models guidelines for good digital citizenship. It establishes a mindset and practice where student actions are judged not on compliance to a restrictive set of rules, but on what is acceptable and appropriate. Let's take a closer look at some specific guidelines that make up this model.

Digital Citizenship Agreements for Students

Since our Global Digital Citizen Foundation first published digital citizenship agreements under the Creative Commons license, we have looked on as thousands of schools have used them as foundations for their own program. Creative Commons is a nonprofit organization that aims to increase the volume of work available in the public domain. It is free and legal to share and repurpose works published under Creative Commons (Creative Commons, n.d.).

In this section, we present several digital citizenship agreements available under Creative Commons license for primary, middle, and high schools, along with commentary on why each guideline is important. We present full, uncommented versions of these agreements in appendix C (page 143), which you may use and change as you see fit. You can also go to **go.SolutionTree.com/technology** or the Resources section of the Global Digital Citizen Foundation website (https://globaldigitalcitizen.org) to freely view and download them.

Note that there are guidelines in each of these agreements that rely on your understanding of *information fluency*. This is a concept of student understanding that defines a student's ability to interpret information, extract knowledge from it, and perceive its meaning and significance (Crockett & Churches, 2017). Developing information fluency is a process that begins in primary school and is something your digital citizenship guidelines can stimulate and nurture. Let's begin with the primary school agreement.

Primary School Agreement

The primary (elementary) school digital citizenship agreement is simply worded as a series of *I will* and *I will not* statements that primary school students can understand. These statements address students taking steps to look after themselves and others while online, as well as establish the importance of respecting property. Unlike the other agreements in this chapter, this one does not include a place for students to sign because, at this level, students do not have a proper understanding of the implications of using a signature to agree to terms.

Looking After Myself

I will only go on the computer when I have permission.

> **Why is this important?** Seeking permission from teachers or parents teaches students a few crucial concepts. First, they learn to be mindful about sharing property with others (as will often be the case with school technology). Second, they gain a sense of how to properly manage their technology time, as opposed to just wasting time on the computer.

I will only go to pages I am allowed to go to.

> **Why is this important?** Students must adhere to policies regarding which pages are safe to visit. The teacher should make a list of both safe and unsafe pages. This helps students gain an awareness of the fact that there is unsafe or inappropriate content online. It encourages a sense of discipline and

self-regulation as they do online work. These same practices easily translate to home environments.

I will only share pictures and stories about myself when my teacher tells me to.

Why is this important? This helps students understand that only certain things about themselves should be shared online. Both teachers and parents can help guide students to understanding what would be considered too much information. The idea is that they learn self-discipline and self-regulation when sharing information about themselves. Preserving a good digital footprint by only posting acceptable information and not something that may hurt them in the future—chances for employment or acceptance into a college or university, for example—is essential.

I will talk to my parents and teacher about all of my online friends.

Why is this important? It's crucial that both teachers and parents know the people students are interacting with online. This guides students to an awareness of the importance of knowing who they are connecting with using social media (and other means) because sometimes people online aren't who they make themselves out to be.

I will tell my teacher or parents if anyone is unkind to me on the computer.

Why is this important? The more students raise awareness about abusive online behaviors, the more likely parents and teachers are to take steps to work together in acting out against them. Telling adults about it shows students that it is not okay to abuse and insult people online. It teaches them to always be respectful, and teachers and parents can guide students toward an awareness of how abusive online behavior can hurt other people and bring consequences to the abuser. Students also need to know which people and groups they can go to for safety and support should they become victims themselves.

Looking After Others

I will only say nice things about people.

Why is this important? By practicing this every day, students learn how to exercise the capacity they have to empower others through warmth, kindness, and sensitivity.

I will ask before I share a picture or story about a person.

Why is this important? This is all about teaching the importance of respecting other people's privacy and personal boundaries. Parents and teachers can guide students to an awareness of how posting information about others online without their consent can be hurtful and disrespectful.

I will only go to places that are nice, and I will tell my parents or teacher if I go to a place that is nasty, unkind, or rude.

> **Why is this important?** Accidentally visiting an online (or offline) environment that is nasty or unkind can be damaging to young children. The sooner parents and teachers know about it, the sooner they can provide necessary counseling and direction, and help the student understand what happened. In this way, students learn to be safe and can also learn the importance of warning their friends not to go to these bad online places.

Looking After Property

I will not download movies, games, or music.

> **Why is this important?** Students get an awareness of how easily intellectual property can be stolen and shared. This guideline offers them an introduction to digital piracy.

I will check that the information I get online is correct.

> **Why is this important?** Teachers and parents can capitalize on students' natural sense of curiosity and growing reading skills by teaching basic research and fact checking, which are parts of information fluency. Students can learn to link topics to keywords and search for patterns in multiple sources to begin to see how online information can separate fact from fiction.

I will not leave rude or unkind messages on other people's spaces.

> **Why is this important?** Students learn the value of receiving and giving constructive and encouraging comments to people who share their creativity. It teaches students to treat others the way they want to be treated when they work hard to produce something they are proud of and want to share with a larger community.

Middle School Agreement

The middle school digital citizenship agreement increases the complexity of its guidelines over that of the primary school agreement. It reflects the students' growing social world in a way that gives them freedom to form new bonds and friendships and explore new worlds of information, but still requires them to take steps to look after themselves and others and show an increasing awareness of and respect for property. This agreement does include a student signature, not to make it binding in a legal sense, but to establish the connection of responsibility to signing an agreement.

Looking After Myself

I will choose online names that are suitable and respectful.

Why is this important? How students represent themselves online can make a big difference in their professional or educational pursuits, since potential employers and administrators use social media for profile checks. This practice shows that students have dignity and self-respect and are willing to represent themselves in a positive light in their online networks.

I will only invite people I actually know in the physical world to be my friends in the online world.

Why is this important? People do not always present themselves online as they really are. Knowing the people students connect with online makes them much safer candidates for building online relationships that involve safe sharing and collaboration practices. Friends are more likely to work to protect each other and tell each other if what one of them is doing is risky or inappropriate.

I will only visit sites that are appropriate, and I will respect the rules that websites have about age. Some sites are only for adults. If I don't feel comfortable showing the website to my parents or grandparents, then it is inappropriate.

Why is this important? This practice sets healthy boundaries for web browsing, and it could help keep students safe from potential emotional or psychological trauma from visiting an inappropriate site. The practice of respecting website rules also develops students' discipline and respectful mindsets.

I will set my privacy settings so only the people I know can see me or my personal information.

Why is this important? This prevents anyone unknown to the student from viewing his or her personal information, which helps keep him or her safer from prowlers, bullies, or Internet trolls.

I will only put information online that is appropriate and post only pictures that are suitable. Not everyone seeing my profile or pictures will be friendly.

Why is this important? This practice helps remind students about their digital footprints, and how portraying themselves online can affect their chances for future employment or enrollment in postsecondary institutions. It reminds students that protecting themselves from undesired attention from potentially harmful observers online is a crucial practice for staying safe.

I will always report anything that happens online that makes me feel uncomfortable or unhappy.

Why is this important? Students must be clear that if they feel threatened or unsafe online, they don't have to just take it. There are people they can go to, and there is support they can receive. In such cases, parents and teachers should determine and organize safe people or groups for students to go to.

I will talk to trusted adults, like my parents and teachers, about my online experiences. This includes both the good and the bad experiences.

> **Why is this important?** Talking about online experiences helps develop the trust triangle between parents, teachers, and students. Being upfront with trusted adults about online experiences helps students gain a sense of support, knowledge, and guidance from more experienced individuals.

Looking After Others

I will show I care by not flaming (sending hurtful or inflammatory messages) other people, or forwarding messages that are unkind or inappropriate.

> **Why is this important?** This teaches students how to comment on the work and efforts of others in inspiring ways. In collaborative settings, it can help students develop the practice of giving constructive criticism. As far as digital interactions go, students will become aware that not everyone online has good intentions, and it helps them develop an awareness of what trolling, flaming, and cyberbullying can do to harm others.

I will not get involved in conversations that are unkind, mean, or bullying.

> **Why is this important?** It's important for students to realize that giving their attention and energy to such discussions only encourages them to continue, and perhaps even spiral harmfully out of control.

I will report any conversations I see that are unkind, mean, or bullying. I can imagine if the things being written were about me. If I find them offensive, then they are inappropriate.

> **Why is this important?** Reporting such behavior guides students toward setting an example for themselves and their peers that abusive environments are unwelcome and won't be tolerated.

I will show my respect for others by avoiding websites that are disrespectful because they show people behaving inappropriately or illegally—or are racist, bigoted, or unkind. If I visit one by accident, I will close it and tell my teacher or an adult.

> **Why is this important?** Staying away from these kinds of sites encourages a mindset for safe online practices. It guides students to understand that the less people collectively view such sites, the better the chances of them being discontinued or taken down. It's a passive, yet extremely powerful way for students to act out against racism and prejudice.

I will show respect for others' privacy by not trying to get into their online spaces without invitation, and by not stalking them or copying their pictures.

> **Why is this important?** This teaches students about personal boundaries and respecting the intellectual property of others. It promotes respectful behavior toward everyone online, regardless of whether the student knows them or not.

Looking After Property

I will not steal other people's property. It's easy to download music, games, and movies, but piracy (downloading media that I have not bought) is just the name given to stealing online.

> **Why is this important?** Students must be made aware that even though it seems harmless, and even though it only happens in a few seconds with the click of a mouse, the fact is that piracy is still theft. It is still a crime. Students must be made aware that anonymity in illegal downloading, or any other type of inappropriate online behavior, should not be considered a guarantee of safety from potential consequences.

I will not share with other people the music, movies, games, and other software that I own.

> **Why is this important?** Sharing properties that students own with others is another form of piracy, since it's technically a duplication of what they own being created without being paid for. Note that this does not apply to sharing physical media. It is generally legal and ethically acceptable, for example, to share with a friend a disc containing media, so long as neither party duplicates or stores the data it contains.

I will check that the information I use is correct. Anyone can say anything on the web, so I need to use reliable websites to check that my research is correct. When in doubt, I will ask my teacher or parents.

> **Why is this important?** This teaches students to always check facts and sources when using information. They learn how to properly research and cite all information sources. It stresses the importance and value of information fluency and how to properly apply it in their work.

I will look after other people's websites, acting appropriately when visiting them, not making changes or vandalizing them, and reporting any damage that I find.

> **Why is this important?** This encourages respect for other people's work and intellectual property. It guides students toward adopting a supportive mindset when visiting sites that they like and want to share with their friends and family.

High School Agreement

The high school digital citizenship agreement further increases complexity by combining sets of ideas into paragraph-length guidelines. It also features a broader set of categories that frame the guidelines around the essential practices of respect and responsibility. These guidelines reflect that students in this age group have increasing independence and the sophistication to think through and make responsible choices with only limited oversight. At this point, students should recognize the significance and impact of signing their names to contracts.

Respect for Myself

I will show respect for myself through my actions. I will select online names that are appropriate. I will consider the information and images I post online. I will not post personal information about my life, experiences, experimentation, or relationships. I will not be obscene.

> **Why is this important?** How students represent themselves online can make a big difference in their professional or educational pursuits, since potential employers and administrators use social media for profile checks. These practices show that the students have dignity and self-respect and wish to represent themselves in the best light possible. It demonstrates that students genuinely care about their future.

Responsibility for Myself

I will ensure that the information I post online will not put me at risk. I will not publish my personal details, contact details, or a schedule of my activities. I will report any attacks or inappropriate behavior directed at me. I will protect passwords, accounts, and resources.

> **Why is this important?** Students must learn to keep themselves safe in online environments. Publishing personal details can be risky, since unsavory individuals can use that information for damaging purposes. It's important that students also do everything they can to ensure that such behavior is decisively acted against. Students must realize it is a conscious decision to do nothing and let the behavior continue or to stand up and do something. This ideal guides students toward deliberately thinking about taking personal password protection seriously.

Respect for Others

I will show respect to others. I will not use electronic mediums to flame, bully, harass, or stalk other people. I will show respect for other people in my choice of websites. I will not visit sites that are degrading, pornographic, racist, or inappropriate. I will not abuse my rights of access, and I will not enter other people's private spaces or areas.

> **Why is this important?** The world has enough bullies. Students can show they are above such behavior by treating others with kindness and respect online and offline. Also, the places students go online make up part of their digital footprint, which can be hard or impossible to permanently erase. Because the sites people visit say a lot about them, students must carefully govern where they go online. Having Internet access is a privilege, not a right. People are fortunate to be able to search online for anything they want and to have the web entertain them. Thus, rights of access are gifts everyone must respect for the good of everyone.

Responsibility for Others

I will protect others by reporting abuse, not forwarding inappropriate materials or communications, and not visiting sites that are degrading, pornographic, racist, or inappropriate.

> **Why is this important?** Insomuch as students should report wrongs done to them, students should do the same for others. It establishes a sense of community when everyone protects and cares for each other online and offline. What is encouraged continues, and what is discouraged fades. Not forwarding inappropriate and degrading material lets the perpetrators know that students will not give energy or consideration to such behavior and helps reduce its proliferation.

Respect for Property

I will request permission to use resources. I will suitably cite any and all use of websites, books, media, and so on. I will acknowledge all primary and secondary sources. I will validate information. I will use and abide by fair-use rules.

> **Why is this important?** The Internet is full of content that people have worked hard to put there, and it is important to respect their efforts. Citing and acknowledging sources is good online community–building practice. It lets others know students appreciate and honor the knowledge they provide. Unfortunately, not all that information is useful. Practicing information fluency skills helps students determine credible sources and which are risky or ungenuine.

Responsibility for Property

I will request to use the software and media others produce. I will use free and open-source alternatives rather than pirating software. I will purchase, license, and register all software. I will purchase my music and other media, and refrain from distributing these in a manner that violates their licenses. I will act with integrity.

Why is this important? Students should learn to take advantage of open-source media because there is so much fantastic license-free content out there that creators have submitted for general use. That said, taking steps toward properly requesting permission to use others' work shows a level of respect and consideration that is both professionally and personally meaningful. This could also lead students to consider generously sharing some of their own work.

Students should memorize these three words: *Piracy is theft*. Piracy has never been a victimless crime, despite what we're led to believe. Piracy costs the entertainment industry billions of dollars and people's jobs every year. For example, a study published at the Social Science Research Network estimates that from 2006 to 2008 alone the Motion Picture Association of America lost 15 percent ($1.3 billion) of its revenue to online piracy (Ma, Montgomery, & Smith, 2016).

Purpose and Customization

These open digital citizenship agreements address almost all the outcomes a school should strive to achieve. With your advance team, look at the defined purposes and determine if these documents address your desired outcomes. In cases where these terms do not work for your school, make changes that adhere to its unique culture.

The following chapters focus on developing the various stakeholder communities to foster global digital citizenship. In the next chapter, we begin with developing the teaching community.

Guiding Questions

As you reflect on this chapter, consider the following four guiding questions.

1. How has BYOD changed the state of educational technology in your schools? What challenges must your school overcome?

2. How are you currently using technology in your own classrooms?

3. What is the most effective way to use technology to move learning forward?

4. How would you evaluate your current acceptable use policy or digital citizenship agreement?

chapter 4

Developing the Teaching Community

There are three stakeholder communities involved in developing and supporting digital citizenship guidelines: (1) the student community, (2) the teaching community, and (3) the wider community, which includes parents, boards of trustee members, businesses, and so on. In our experience, these guidelines are most successful when all three stakeholder groups develop, agree on, and practice the guidelines themselves.

This means that parents and teachers also sign digital citizenship agreements and pledge to hold themselves to the same standards as students. For example, once the stakeholder communities agree on the consequence for downloading illegal content such as movies, music, and games (the digital equivalent of theft), the consequence will apply to teachers and parents as well. In our experience, the most effective way to develop a set of steps and escalation is to mirror the consequences for actions in the physical world. If theft constitutes expulsion or police involvement with physical property, it should apply equally to downloading pirated movies and games as well.

Once your advance team is prepared to move forward, the next step is to engage the various stakeholder communities in the process. This chapter outlines what this work should include within the teaching community, including the following.

- The distinction between how children and adults learn (or *andragogy* versus *pedagogy*)
- The unique role the teaching profession has in students' lives and what makes teachers critical role models
- Our guidance for achieving buy-in from teachers
- Some notable characteristics of adult learners

We begin by exploring the differences between how young and adult learners learn and why you need a different, tailored approach for teachers.

Andragogy Versus Pedagogy

Adults and children don't learn in the same way; approaches that work for one community don't necessarily resonate with the other. Teachers are practitioners of *pedagogy*, which is the art and science of teaching—specifically, teaching *children* (for our purposes). Students value boundaries and clear guidelines. But, as young people progress toward adulthood and increase their independence, how they learn changes (Knowles, 1980).

Enter, *andragogy*, which is the art and science of helping adults learn (Knowles, 1980). Andragogy requires a markedly different approach than the pedagogical approaches teachers employ with child learners. As you can see from the descriptors, the emphasis is different, with pedagogy focused on *teaching* and andragogy focused on *helping*.

There is a risk when teachers employ the same pedagogical models with peers that they use with students, rather than employing andragogical principles. Malcolm S. Knowles, in his 1980 work *The Modern Practice of Adult Education: From Pedagogy to Andragogy*, compares the basics of pedagogy to andragogy—child learning to adult learning (see table 4.1).

Table 4.1: Differences Between Pedagogy and Andragogy

Pedagogy	Andragogy
The young learner is dependent on the teacher.	The adult learner prefers to be responsible for their own learning.
The young learner brings limited experience to the learning situation.	The adult learner has accumulated a wide and rich range of experiences.
The young learner is often externally motivated.	The adult learner is often internally motivated.
The young learner prefers subject-oriented learning.	The adult learner prefers problem-centered learning.
The young learner accepts learning without a broader context.	The adult learner needs to understand the reason and importance of their learning.

Source: Adapted from International Baccalaureate, 2014; Knowles, 1980.

The shift from pedagogy to andragogy is a continuum. As the young learner matures and develops, the approaches to learning move to encompass more adult-based approaches. Younger learners do not require explanations of the significance and importance their learning holds. They like learning to be conveniently packaged into easy-to-work-with, bite-size parcels, so teaching discrete subjects suits them. They thrive on the encouragement and enthusiasm of their teachers. But as they mature, young learners begin to ask, "Why? Why is this significant? Why is this important?" They like to see the links between areas of learning. They are shifting and maturing toward a more adult form of learning, and the teaching approaches need to change to suit the changing needs of learners.

There is no clear point when to swap from pedagogy to andragogy, but what we know as mature adult learners is that we are responsible for our own learning, and that we motivate ourselves to learn. If the learning does not have relevance and context we, like older students, are less likely to fully engage in the process. This is why shaping your teachers' approach to global digital citizenship requires a different approach from educating students.

The Critical Role Model

In many professions, there is a clear demarcation between work life and home life. Work is left at work. When workers in many other professions clock out for the day, their work day ends, and their separate home life begins.

Teaching is not one of those professions. Teaching is a profession based around caring, because teachers have care and concerns for their young charges, and that care and concern do not stop at the day-ending bell. It is a profession where students, peers, the community, and the board look at teachers as role models. This scrutiny goes beyond their performance as teachers and encompasses all aspects of their lives.

Each group also has an expectation that a teacher's behavior and conduct have exceptionally high standards. The expectation, which is on par with other caring professions like medical professions, extends to a level where the actions of teachers beyond school can and sometimes will impact their employment. Teaching is a 24-7-365 profession, and, as many teachers have found out, posting materials to social media can sometimes be fraught with danger. Posts, although witty and humorous at the time, may reflect poorly on a teacher—a reflection that extends to the school. The result is sometimes part of the law of unexpected consequences, in which otherwise innocuous or innocent behavior comes with negative consequences for the individual posting the content. Genuinely inappropriate actions are viewed even more dimly.

So, teachers are role models at school and beyond. Many teachers have had the great pleasure of former students recalling to them how their class and teaching shaped their lives and employment. Some have had the ultimate compliment of students citing them as a reason why they became teachers. Does this perhaps mean the inverse is also true, whereby negative student-to-teacher experiences harm a student's future? As a profession, these young charges look up to teachers, and their actions—sadly, also their inactions—profoundly influence and impact students.

Most of us that work in education know from developmental psychology that teachers have students in class at critical times in the evolution of their ethical and moral beliefs and understandings (Kohlberg, 2008). We have the proof of this ourselves. If we reflect on our own time in school, we will see in our mind's eye the teachers who helped shape us into the education professionals that we are. We can recall the impact they had, the passion they fueled for a subject, and our essential understanding of it.

Thus, it is in our world of connectivity, immediacy, and change that teachers still hold a critical role. They fuel the desire to learn and the passion for a subject, and provide the role models for acceptable and appropriate behavior.

Teachers are even role models beyond the classroom. When teachers go out for an evening, it is common for them to encounter students. They judge the teachers' actions and often shape their own based on what they see teachers do. Similarly, students view, appraise, and evaluate what teachers post online. Students make judgments based on the superficial appearance of a post, photo, or media clip without the context and background that the teachers' friends may have. Therefore, your digital citizenship agreements must apply to faculty and students alike. However, if these agreements are to apply to teachers, that means providing teachers with the support they require, including crafting a digital citizenship agreement that is grounded in sound andragogical principles.

Guidance for Teachers

Schools, as institutions, are great at providing advice for students. Schools frequently clarify expectations of student behavior, advise them on vocational pathways, and provide detailed and in-depth support on a huge range of matters. However, schools seldom provide adequate support and guidance for teachers, particularly regarding the use of the diverse forms of information and communication technologies that abound today.

There is almost an expectation of innate knowledge and understanding of the latest developments in digital mediums, much like the misplaced expectations that all young people are inherently talented and skilled in the use of computers, smart devices, and the like. Teachers also need support and guidance if they are to provide appropriate and timely advice to enthusiastic preteens and inquiring and exploring adolescents.

Working with the teaching community takes a twofold approach. The teachers need support and guidance on what is acceptable and suitable behavior for themselves, and equally important, they need to understand and justify the school community's stance in guiding students in their digital interactions. Specifically, this section addresses the following topics.

- The argument for guidelines rather than rules
- A professional digital citizenship agreement for teachers
- Social media as friend or foe
- Pitfalls of not adhering to guidelines
- Pitfalls of assumed knowledge

We begin with the importance of establishing guidelines rather than rules.

The Argument for Guidelines Rather Than Rules

We write extensively in this book about how traditional acceptable use policies work mainly as a set of rules and regulations for what is and isn't acceptable behavior, with backing from legal counsel. These policies lack context and relevance, but nonetheless require blind agreement and adherence from teachers. This goes against all principles of andragogy.

Andragogic principles require a compelling argument and guidelines that provide context and relevance that link to the teacher's own life experiences. This provides teachers with internal motivation to learn, adapt, and change their behavior to effect better outcomes for both themselves and the students they serve.

A strict set of rules and regulations also ignores fundamental technological realities. Because they focus on location rather than behavior, rules that rely on banning the use of an application or website are fundamentally flawed and obsolete. Consider the rapid evolution of web apps, smartphone apps, and application development. The Google Play online store, which started as the Android Market in December 2009, reached its first million applications in July 2013 (Statista, n.d.b). Just three years later, the Google Play online store reached 2.2 million applications (Statista, n.d.b). Figure 4.1 is testimony to the rapid development and deployment of these software packages and the significance of smartphones.

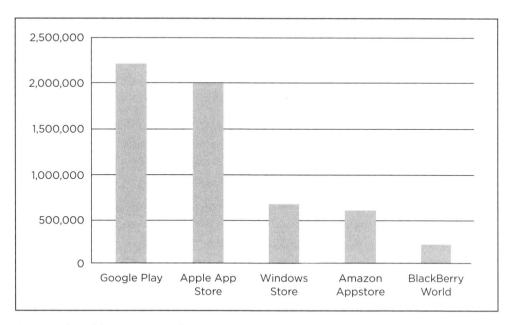

Source: Adapted from Statista, n.d.a.

Figure 4.1: Graph of applications available in each of the major app stores as of July 2016.

Likewise, the *Daily Mail* reports in 2014 that the Internet is home to more than one billion websites, and that every second a user registers a new site (Woollaston, 2014).

Because there is no site- or application-based policy that can keep up with this kind of growth, instead of implementing one-size-fits-no-one's rules, providing ethically driven guidance and guidelines on what is and is not acceptable is a more sustainable approach. It is a focus on behavior (what people do) rather than location (where people go or which sites they visit). Focusing on behavior is more encompassing, supportive, adaptable, and beneficial for all. This means presenting teachers with an applicable, behavior-based digital citizenship agreement that is consistent with your student agreements (like those in chapter 3), but with an andragogical approach.

A Professional Digital Citizenship Agreement for Teachers

When teachers present digital citizenship guidelines to students, they *teach* a balanced case for each point. If you are in the position to present digital citizenship guidelines to other teachers, it is important that you draw on these adult learners' rich and diverse experiences to *help* them understand the importance of adopting sound use practices. It is often left unspoken that unacceptable or inappropriate technology use, even on the teachers' own time, can have severe impacts. This is unfair. The teaching community does need to have the significance of digital citizenship clearly brought to the fore. But, like all teachers do for students, each of the guidelines you present to the staff needs to be supported with a considered and reasoned rationale.

Staff guidelines are a logical extension of students' guidelines. Like the high school–level guidelines, staff guidelines are based on respect and responsibility for oneself, others, and property. Getting staff buy-in, however, requires a different presentation. For example, after developing an initial set of professional technology use guidelines, Andrew needed to present them to the staff. In preparation, he printed the guidelines page on large A3 sheets, like those illustrated in figure 4.2, and liberally distributed them around the staffroom where we would meet. (Appendix C, page 143, includes a reproducible version of this digital citizenship agreement.) He prepared a presentation covering the different sections of the guidelines, and for each guideline, he prepared a series of points on the rationale for supporting it.

When Andrew presented these guidelines to the staff as a working document, rather than a completed document, and asked them to provide feedback on printed copies, he assured the staff that he would value and consider their feedback and suggestions. He made sure to tell them that this was "our document" and that "we are preparing for our own safety."

Digital Citizenship Professional Guidelines

Respect for myself by

- Showing respect for myself through my actions

- Considering the information and images that I post online and how these may reflect on myself, my family, and my company

- Considering what personal information about my life, experiences, experimentation, or relationships I post

- Not being obscene, degrading, rude, or inappropriate

Responsibility for myself by

- Considering the impact of my actions and behaviors and consequences of my actions on myself, my family, and my company

- Separating my personal and professional use of technology

- Protecting my identity; ensuring that the information, images, and materials I post online will not put me at risk

- Considering the personal and professional information I have published and that the audience may be broader and wider than I intended

- Taking suitable steps to ensure my online safety and protecting the integrity and security of my data

- Reporting any attacks or inappropriate behavior directed at me and seeking support from appropriate people or organizations

- Protecting passwords, bank and credit card accounts, and resources

- Being aware of the consequences of my actions

Respect for others by

- Using professional language and judgment when sending emails, posts, or messages—even when angry

- Selecting appropriate mediums for my communications, showing consideration to others, and understanding the limitations of different mediums

- Not using electronic mediums to flame, bully, harass, or stalk other people

- Being conscientious in my choice of websites and avoiding, whenever possible, sites that are inappropriate (for example, sites that are degrading, pornographic, or racist)

- Not abusing my rights of access; avoiding entering private spaces or using surveillance systems in a manner that abuses privacy

Figure 4.2: Digital citizenship—professional guidelines. continued →

Responsibility for others by

- Protecting others by reporting abuse and not forwarding inappropriate materials or communications

- Moderating unacceptable materials and conversations and reporting conversations that are inappropriate or unacceptable

- Taking appropriate steps to ensure the safety and privacy of my colleagues and clients; seeking permission before posting their personal and corporate information

- Ensuring that the information held in trust is suitably protected and only used for its intended purpose, and then disposing of said information appropriately

- Limiting access to information to those who legitimately need it, and protecting it from others; refraining from passing said information to third parties

Respect for property by

- Requesting permission to use resources; respecting and abiding by copyright, intellectual property, and patent

- Citing any and all use of websites, books, and other media and acknowledging all primary and secondary sources

- Validating information

- Being transparent in my licensing of software, media, and materials

Responsibility for property by

- Maintaining professional awareness of my rights to use other people's material

- Suitably protecting my and my company's copyright, intellectual property, and patent

- Using appropriately obtained, licensed, and registered software and media

- Using media within the limitations of their licenses and refraining from distributing these in a manner that violates these conditions

- Suitably protecting my systems to ensure their security and integrity

- Reporting vandalism and damage

By signing this agreement, I undertake to always act in a manner that is respectful to myself and others, and to act appropriately and in a moral and ethical manner.

I, _____, agree to follow the principles of digital citizenship outlined in this agreement and accept that failing to follow these tenets will have consequences.

Signed: _____

Date: _____ / _____ / _____

Not only did teachers receive this approach well, but the feedback on guidelines was useful and insightful, pointing out not only grammatical errors but also further refinements. Their input gave the staff ownership of their shared guidelines as well as a much richer and deeper understanding of digital citizenship and the potential consequences of their actions.

For teachers, signing on to these sorts of digital citizenship guidelines often raises questions, particularly with regard to what they should or shouldn't do when using social media.

Social Media as Friend or Foe

Social media sometimes has a bad rap. It is a great medium for learning, collaborating, and communicating. It is a medium students and staff are often comfortable in, and this familiarity can make communication and interaction easy. That said, sometimes familiarity leads to contempt.

Many schools have a social media–based platform to leverage learning. These platforms, which focus on education, enable structure and process while providing a safe and controlled environment for students to learn the appropriate methods of interacting online. We often refer to this type of platform as a *walled garden*. It is when social media interactions move beyond the safety of this walled garden at school and into the physical world that the boundaries, conventions, and protocols fall away. As such, teachers can inadvertently find themselves in compromising situations.

Being friends with or following students on social media outside of the school's mediums is a risk-filled business. Much of young people's lives is lived out, revisited, and replayed in their profile updates and photo and video streams. As connected friends on social media, their activities, posts, and actions can compromise teachers. It is easy for outsiders and insiders alike to misinterpret or misconstrue a response to their comments or a student's responses to teachers' posts. A comment that may have been heavily based in irony in a verbal context may be seen literally in a text form.

Even discounting this inevitability, unfortunately, friendship does not motivate all teachers' interactions online. We have seen some teachers who have taken advantage of the privileged position they hold and used it to gain and abuse the trust of students.

Between the deliberate inappropriate relationships and the ease with which outsiders often misinterpret conversations, as well as the access to materials that should be kept private for both parties, we do not advise forming online student-teacher friendships.

Pitfalls of Not Adhering to Guidelines

Although the guidelines in our digital citizenship agreements are just that—guidelines—sticking to them is something that benefits students and teachers alike. Consider the story of Douglas, an experienced and skilled teacher of digital technologies. When Douglas prepares his lessons, he often uses slide-based tools to present the key points. As he has said on several occasions, students are not drawn to a slide full of text, but rather to exciting and relevant images. Because he is modeling appropriate and ethical behavior, Douglas sources his images by selecting the usage rights option in his Google search (see figure 4.3, page 70). He always acknowledges the image source on the bottom right-hand corner of the slides.

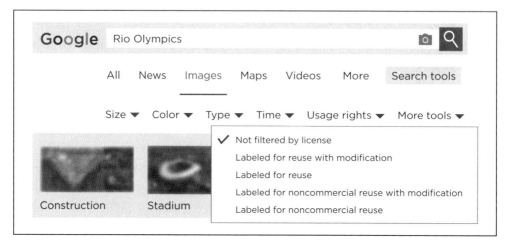

Source: Google and the Google logo are registered trademarks of Google Inc. Used with permission.

Figure 4.3: An example of Creative Commons usage rights within Google search tools.

Douglas's habit of acknowledging and giving suitable credit for image sources, as well as only using images marked for reuse, has led to several interesting conversations among staff and students alike regarding what is appropriate for accessing and using images.

Douglas's example highlights the importance of the teacher's role in all aspects of digital citizenship guidelines. Imagine what happens if he does not take this step. The teacher who ignores one part of the guidelines—for example, *being responsible for property by using only appropriately obtained, licensed, and registered software and media*—undermines the importance of the others. Students will quickly think that if this part isn't that important, then neither are others.

Search engines like Google often make it easier to grab the nicest image that appears in a search rather than use the advanced tools to ethically source pictures and graphics. Do not succumb to cutting corners in this way. It is a simple step to select the usage rights option and pick an image labeled for reuse.

A key role for teachers is the requirement to ethically source and acknowledge the sources of media and information into assessment and classroom tasks. For example, Wikimedia Commons, part of the Wikipedia group of sites, contains over thirty-two million media files that fall under the Creative Commons license. Select one and use it!

Consistently adhering to digital citizenship agreement guidelines isn't the only pitfall, of course. Teachers bear not only responsibility for sticking to the guidelines but also making sure their students truly understand them. There is nothing more frustrating for the teacher and students than the expectation that students know something, when the harsh reality is that they don't.

Pitfalls of Assumed Knowledge

It can be dangerous for teachers to assume students have knowledge that they may, in fact, not possess. For example, imagine that a teacher asks students to develop a bibliography of resources used in an assignment. The results range from URLs (or web addresses) copied and pasted quickly into the final page of the assignment to a bibliography using American Psychological Association or Modern Language Association formatting. In other words, the results are inconsistent, and the inconsistency frustrates both the teacher and students.

Many teachers expect students have been taught certain key skills in other classes. These are the transferable skills students can apply in a variety of situations across a range of subjects. The skill of information fluency, where the development of suitable techniques for bibliographies and acknowledging sources fits, is one of these (Crockett, Jukes, & Churches, 2011). The reality is that we are all teachers of the different fluencies and digital citizenship. Teaching these key skills is easier if the school selects one standard approach that everyone uses. At the same time, there must be an adequate on-boarding process to ensure students who come to the school, either through normal grade progressions or mid-year transfers, fully understand the process.

This obviously applies to most, if not all, transferable skills. Selecting common approaches and developing a common language for assessment and digital citizenship reduce each teacher's workload and ensure students receive a common and uniform message about what is important and what the school's expectations are.

Approaches to Adult Development

As you have seen throughout this chapter, how teachers approach adult teaching and learning is markedly different from how they facilitate student teaching and learning. It is the difference between pedagogy and andragogy. Leaders and coaches need to apply the principles of andragogy to support teachers in actively modeling and teaching digital citizenship.

Characteristics of adult learners include the following.

- Need to see the relevance and context for learning
- Can draw on their broad range of experiences
- Are internally motivated
- Like to be responsible for their own learning

Never forget that teachers are active role models and have a huge influence on the development of students well beyond the students' time in the classroom. Make sure the messages, skills, processes, and morals you teach students are the best they can be. Teach ethically!

Next up, we look at what's involved in developing the student community.

Guiding Questions

As you reflect on this chapter, consider the following five guiding questions.

1. Why are parents and teachers, as well as middle school and high school students, encouraged to sign a school's digital citizenship agreements?

2. Explain the fundamental differences in meaning and approach between *pedagogy* and *andragogy*.

3. What role does andragogy play in implementing a digital citizenship agreement in a school?

4. What are the dangers of a teacher adopting a social media friendship with a student?

5. What are the benefits of adopting a common language across the school when teaching digital citizenship?

chapter 5

Developing the Student Community

In chapter 4, we introduced the idea that there are three stakeholder communities involved in developing and supporting guidelines. That chapter focused on the teaching community, while chapter 6 focuses on the wider community. In this chapter, we write in detail about the needs of the student community: why leased device programs are problematic and BYOD is a revelation. We also offer guidance for achieving student buy-in and why it's critical to establish partnerships outside school. Note that because we provide detailed analyses of student digital citizenship guidelines in chapter 3, we do not include them here. You can also find full, reproducible sets of all digital citizenship guidelines in appendix C.

Leased Devices

In 1990, Methodist Ladies' College in Melbourne, Australia, became the first school in the world to start a one-to-one laptop program (Johnstone, 2003). They began with the fifth-grade students, with the shared understanding that providing laptops to the students would be empowering (Johnstone, 2003). In the same year, Sir Tim Berners-Lee, working at CERN (European Organization for Nuclear Research) in Switzerland, wrote the first web client and server, which would later become a web browser (World Wide Web Consortium, 2016).

These two events started an avalanche, by shifting the face of education. No longer is the teacher the primary source of information and the gateway to learning. Each of us, student and teacher alike, has direct access to the sum total of human knowledge. This has irrevocably disrupted education's structure and methods. The adoption of BYOD programs, a term Intel first used in 2009 to describe how their employees were connecting their personal devices to the company's network ("Bring your own device," n.d.), has only accelerated this avalanche.

Because the first one-to-one programs provided the students with laptops leased from the school, the school held ownership of the laptop, provided the software, and set the restrictions on what could or could not be done, often quite vigorously. Device ownership residing with the school also meant that the school legally had the right to access the devices, and this later resulted in many schools instigating apparently random checks to find students who infringed the schools' acceptable use policies (Patchin, 2011). Through these managed laptop programs, schools could maintain very strict control over technology. Some schools even went to the extent of hiring former police officers to oversee the use or potential misuse of the devices. This type of police state does little to support student learning, and sometimes harms it. Curiosity is an essential component of learning, and this type of environment is not conducive to curiosity and exploration.

Device restrictions often have unexpected consequences that can frustrate students, including the inability to personalize the device, and what the students see as a lack of flexibility. There are also long-duration leases (some up to four years), and this is particularly problematic because as lease duration increases, so does damage from wear and tear. In these scenarios, students become increasingly frustrated as aging devices fail to operate at acceptable levels. In our experience, sometimes students deliberately mistreat devices to attempt to replace it with a faster, better device than the old and slow one. These frustrations stifle creativity, enhance dissatisfaction, and make students, faculty, and parents alike question the relevance and value of using these devices in the classroom.

In our experience, parents often contacted the support staff to request administration rights to connect to networks, install software, and make other changes to a device's configuration. This was the heyday of the IT department. It represents a time when, in many cases, IT managers had supreme control over the school via their control over technology. They often made decisions based on their own needs and whims rather than on the educational significance and importance of the change or requests. We've seen schools blessed with visionary IT managers and staff who did all they could to facilitate education and learning, but others were not as fortunate. This nightmare scenario represents the technical tail wagging the educational dog. Fortunately, BYOD upends the equation.

Bring Your Own Device

BYOD changes the playing field. For example, when Andrew's school rolled out its BYOD program, he saw a surge in the computer use and an equally marked drop in damage. It also had the financial benefit that the school was no longer responsible for maintaining the master lease of a large fleet of laptops or insurance, nor the licensing of the various software applications.

In a step away from what a number of schools had done at that stage, the BYOD requirements the Kristin School set were simple. Students who participate in BYOD need to do the following.

- Connect to the Wi-Fi network
- Connect to the learning management system (which requires a functional web browser)
- Maintain an antivirus application
- Have software that enables using a range of file formats

In the case of file formats, the school lists .doc (Word), .ppt (PowerPoint), .xls (Excel), and .pdf (Adobe), and a variety of other media, audio, and image formats. The school did not select the formats because of a bias toward Microsoft Windows or Office, but rather because most productivity suites—Microsoft Office, Apple iWork, Apache OpenOffice, and Google Docs—can open, edit, and save in these formats.

The original concept and proposal for BYOD involved implementation within a single high school grade level. All students in that grade shifted to the BYOD model. At the time, the school gave the other high school grades the option to bring their own devices for connection.

The uptake was extraordinary. Not only did all the year 11 (grade 10; the initial target grade) students connect, but within three months of BYOD program availability, so did 98 percent of the entire school! Astonishingly, many students took the opportunity to connect multiple devices—their primary learning device (laptops) and also secondary devices (phones and tablets). In 2016, the program extended across both the middle and high schools with over forty-five hundred registered devices for approximately twelve hundred students. This is strong evidence that if you provide students the opportunity, they will seize it with both hands.

Like it did for many schools, the BYOD change at the Kristin School created a new challenge, which by this point in the book you have probably guessed. Control shifted from the traditional model, where the school had control, to a distributed model, where the students and their parents have control. With this change also came a change in the acceptable use policies, and a change in the entire approach to digital citizenship. Gone were the rights of search and seizure that the lease model provided. But even more important, gone was control over the installed software, and with this came a change in required staff skill sets. Instead of teaching the software package, teachers now taught the underlying technology principles of the skill set.

These include principles like the following.

- Graphic design
- Word processing
- Data processing
- Presentations
- File management
- Digital citizenship

The word *principles* is key in this context. The principles in this list are portable in that you can broadly apply them to a range of software and not just to a particular app or product suite. In an age of rapid evolution of productivity suites, with new versions released every couple of years, skills tied to a software package are quickly obsolete, but the principles under which they operate are timeless. The freedom that comes from a successful fundamentals-centered BYOD rollout allows teachers to focus more specifically on the development of students across all ages.

Student Buy-In

In chapter 3, we detailed three different digital citizenship agreements based on school level. The concept of digital citizenship and responsibility must suit the students' ages and maturation and development levels. There are many theories that attempt to explain the different stages that a child progresses through toward adulthood. For example, many educators have seen or can recognize in students the stages of Erik Erikson's model of psychosocial development. Erikson's stages of psychosocial development (n.d.) often map directly to online behaviors (see table 5.1).

Table 5.1: Stages of Psychosocial Development

Ages	Stage	Characteristics	Behaviors
4–5	Initiative versus guilt	Learning to master the world around them, development of guilt	Learning about technology
5–12	Industry versus inferiority	Responsibility, play, development of self-confidence and sometimes inferiority	Expanding technology use to use common tools like search engines
12–18	Identity versus confusion	Exploration, experimentation, development of sexual identity, identity crisis, development of personal ideologies	Surfing pornography, contributing to social media groups, cyberbullying

Source: Adapted from Erikson's stages of psychosocial development, n.d.

Teachers also need to consider the young person's level of functional literacy. Consider the fictional example of Phoebe. On the first day of school, Phoebe and her mother arrive at school. Phoebe is an excited, confident, and enthusiastic five-year-old. On arrival, the school staff present them with various documents, including a policy-focused acceptable use agreement, which they expected both the mother and daughter to sign. Phoebe's mother dutifully signs the document and passes it to Phoebe, indicating that she has to sign it too. Phoebe writes her name and then hands over the document, beaming with excitement and pride. "Look, Mum," she exclaims in a loud voice, "P-H-O-E-B-E. That's Phoebe. I wrote my name!" The word *Phoebe* was one of the very few words she could understand.

This scenario is problematic for an obvious reason—there is no point in getting a child this young to sign an acceptable use policy he or she can't even read. Further, it is the teacher's responsibility to access technology in the classroom. The legal value of many acceptable use policies is questionable until the student reaches the age of majority. (The student is legally an adult.) However, once students can read and understand the guidelines, there is merit and worth in having them agree to the expectations of care and responsibility.

When we developed our digital citizenship guidelines for the different age groups (see appendix C), we ran each agreement through a readability analysis tool. One we find simple to use, and introduced in chapter 1, is the *simplified measure of goobledygook* readability scale. SMOG gives you the number of education years needed to understand the text (SMOG, n.d.). Another measure is the *Gunning fog index*. In this index, if you get a value of less than eight (years), it is considered to have a near-universal understanding ("Gunning fog index," n.d.). These tools both provide good approximations of how easy your document is to read and understand.

Crafting use agreements that students can comprehend is an essential first step for achieving student buy-in. But it is only a step. To get full and enthusiastic student participation, you need to establish for students the benefits of good digital citizenship. There are multiple strategies you can employ to accomplish that.

Guidance for Students

Even the best-written digital citizenship guidelines (or the best-developed and laid-out classroom resources) are of no use unless there is student buy-in. Just like formative feedback, digital citizenship is a partnership; this means there are benefits to both partners. The question then is, How do you show students the benefits of digital citizenship and the importance of showing both respect and responsibility for themselves, other people, and property? The answer to this question involves providing students with a multifaceted response that takes into consideration their age, clarity of the message, and who the rules are ultimately for, plus establishing the connection between physical-world and virtual-world behaviors and the consequences poor behavior brings.

Age-Appropriate Approaches

The digital citizenship agreement must first be age appropriate for students. Primary school students respond very well to clear boundaries and stated rules, but as young people mature, they start to question the reasons for certain rules. At this point, you need to provide clear explanations and stress the significance of the guidelines.

Clarity

For every guideline, there must be a clear and concise rationale. For example, when you discuss respect for property, the issue of piracy always comes up. The nature of the web means that you can access and download almost any game, video, or music file with considerable ease. Often it is easier to download them from a torrent site (a medium for shared distribution of digital files) than it is to legitimately buy them. So, how do you stress the importance of behaving in an ethical and responsible manner?

The easiest way is to show students a selection of actual physical media. Show them Blu-ray discs, DVDs, or CDs in their plastic cases and then ask them how many people would walk into a store, pick these up, and then walk out with them without paying. Not surprisingly, the students respond that they wouldn't. When asked why, some say that they wouldn't do this because it's stealing and others will probably add (slightly alarmingly) that there is a risk of being caught. The parallel can then be drawn between the virtual and physical worlds. It leads to interesting discussions about what the difference is—if any—and why the perception exists that stealing is wrong, but downloading intellectual property is somehow less wrong or at least more acceptable.

Similarly, another parallel that you can easily draw is online sharing and friendships. For many students, it seems that they use social media as naturally as they talk to their peers. Many teachers have witnessed students standing beside each other or across the room, sending each other short messages. While you might question the logic of this and promote the ease of just talking to each other, students will persist with the puzzling paradox, "Why talk when you can text?"

Many students, while using social media, will attempt to collect as many friends or followers as they can, often in the hundreds. As friends on most of the popular social media sites, they have easy access to each other's status and time lines, photos and videos, and often information from their profiles. Unfortunately, this is often a case of too much information. Since students collect friends almost as a method of keeping score, some of their so-called "friends" are untrustworthy, and sometimes pose a genuine threat.

The parallel that we use is to ask students to look around the room, and then ask who would share with everyone in the group their photo albums, pictures of them on holiday, how they are feeling today, and even their address and contact details. Further, if they wanted a copy of the albums and family videos then they could just take a copy. Most students will say that they would not. In fact, most would find the proposition of their classmates copying and keeping their pictures horrifying. The conversation then leads to the reality of social media, and even time-limited applications like Snapchat, where deleted images can be recovered. When you have clarity, you can move on to the importance of privacy, security, and oversharing.

Their Rules, Not Ours

Although use guidelines start with school or district leadership, that isn't where they should end. For example, although Andrew goes to multiple classes and groups to present the school's guidelines, and the rationales for them, he also strives to avoid making the presentations one-sided. At the Kristin School, each year teachers and administration offer students the opportunity to add to and modify the digital citizenship guidelines. We present the guidelines to groups of students and then invite them to make suggestions, recommend modifications, and offer additions to the documents. We shift the rules ownership from just the school to a shared responsibility, thereby forming a partnership. We distribute these refined and agreed-on statements across the whole community, including staff, students, and parents, with the expectation that what applies at school, applies at home.

Physical World Meets Virtual World

A final facet is making clear parallels between actions in the physical and virtual worlds. This is partly the consequences for actions. Being able to equate online actions with equivalent behaviors in the physical world and addressing consequences equivalently are critical. The boundary between the physical world and virtual world is blurring. As it becomes increasingly difficult to differentiate between the two, the equivalence of the behaviors and consequences will be even more critical. Table 5.2 highlights some equivalencies between the physical and virtual worlds.

Table 5.2: Similarities Between Physical and Virtual Worlds

Physical World	Virtual World
Engaging in off-task behaviors	Engaging in off-task behaviors
Passing notes	Engaging in unacceptable communications
Accessing unacceptable materials	Accessing unacceptable materials
Breaking and entering	Hacking
Vandalizing property	Engaging in cyber-vandalism
Bullying	Cyberbullying
Cheating, plagiarizing, and colluding	Cheating, plagiarizing, and colluding

In Andrew's classroom, students are encouraged to use the best tool for the job. They bring the tools they need to learn, but there are clear guidelines on how they use them. The class understands that the use of any tool, whether it is a laptop, tablet, smartphone, or pencil, is for education. All students bring their primary learning devices, usually laptops, and any desired secondary devices. Almost all students have a smartphone of some kind. Smartphones are integral to their learning process, as students will often take photos of the board and desks. The desks in Andrew's classroom are whiteboard desks, so students write notes on them as they work on various activities. The students know that sending personal text messages, chatting on instant messaging apps, or making phone calls is distracting and detracts from the learning process. Some students place their phones at the front of the class so they are not distracted. If they need them, they ask Andrew if they can use them. The expectations are now so ingrained that the students' phones are always on silent, and they will ask if they can take an incoming call.

The result of this trust-based relationship is that students will also bring in interesting devices. During a series of science lessons, one of the students brought in a VR (virtual reality) device because she had found an interesting VR application that connected with the learning activities. Although this is the goal, reaching this point with your own class also requires having consequences for inappropriate behaviors that make sense.

Consequences for Poor Behavior

The consequences for inappropriate behavior should be age-appropriate for the student, but they should not differentiate between the world (physical or virtual) where it occurred. There needs to be a proper correlation between the student's development age and the expected behaviors. When an adolescent student attempts to access unacceptable material of a sexual nature, there *must* be consequences, as this behavior is inappropriate. However, there needs to be a simultaneous understanding that when a middle or high school student explores his or her sexuality, it is part of his or her natural development. This does not mitigate the inappropriate nature of the action, but it should hardly come as a surprise that young people will behave this way.

One of the consequences teachers often apply for inappropriate behavior on a device is to confiscate that device. In many ways, this is counterproductive. Consider this example: if a student is passing notes by taking a piece of paper and using a pen to scribe the offending note, it is very unlikely the teacher will remove the pen and paper from the student, and with good reason—removing the pen and paper would severely hamper the student's ability to work. You must apply the same logic to the devices the students use to learn. Confiscating the offending device impacts the individual's learning. For many young people, the laptop or tablet is analogous with the pen and paper.

Dealing with unacceptable behavior starts before the behaviors begin. Having clear expectations of technology use and a fair and considered rationale for these expectations is the starting point. Many teachers begin the teaching year by working with students to develop a classroom contract. This brings buy-in and agreement within the class. The process we describe for digital citizenship agreements is the same. It is developing the behavior contract on both a schoolwide level and in classroom-size groups.

Having a meeting at the beginning of the year and developing agreed-on expectations based on the guidelines is an excellent start, but developing the moral and ethical behaviors that are the hallmark of a global digital citizen needs to be ongoing. You need a variety of approaches to keep behaviors at the forefront of students' minds. These approaches include the following.

- Displaying posters with the guidelines in the classroom

- Including guidelines in the school handbook

- Adding digital citizenship hints of the day or week in the school's communications, such as notices and newsletters

- Making the agreements and support material available online

- Having the teacher model acceptable use, and discussing how the guidelines apply to all aspects of learning

- Having expectations of acceptable use integrated into assessment tasks, such as using only Creative Commons–licensed media and appropriately acknowledging sources

- Keeping students actively involved in developing guidelines, resources, and consequences for unacceptable behavior

Acceptable and appropriate technology use cannot start and finish with school. You must also develop partnerships beyond school.

Partnerships Beyond School

Depending on the school level, educators see students for sometimes six or more hours, or just for an hour on most days. Teachers do a huge amount as active role models to shape and nurture appropriate behavior, but they cannot do this alone. Although you can set behavior standards and expectations within the school, you don't want students to leave these actions behind when they walk out at the end of the day. The behaviors educators are teaching are life lessons; they are critical building blocks for employment and success beyond the years of direct influence.

To reinforce these lessons and make them unconscious elements of students' behaviors requires guidance and support from home. To that end, chapter 6 details how you nurture the wider community to reinforce the merits of digital citizenship through parent involvement and education.

Guiding Questions

As you reflect on this chapter, consider the following four guiding questions.

1. What about your students do you need to consider when implementing a digital citizenship agreement, and why are these things important?

2. Why is it important to give students a chance to offer input on the development and implementation of a digital citizenship agreement?

3. How do consequences for behaviors in the virtual world parallel those in the physical world?

4. How can this improve the scope of positive influence digital citizenship guidelines have on students?

chapter 6

Developing the Wider Community

Teaching students to be global digital citizens may be an involved process, but it is also a straightforward one. Students are blank slates, eager to learn. The very nature of teaching compels most teachers to set good examples of global digital citizenship. For parents and the wider community outside school, achieving buy-in for a digital citizenship agreement that reflects the tenets of global digital citizenship is a bit trickier.

Parents often have little or no understanding of the risks and benefits of Internet access and connectivity. They are frequently bombarded with stories of sex offenders stalking children, phishing scams, viruses, and even hackers doxing personal information. In this regard, the World Wide Web is both a blessing and a curse. For parents, providing support and guidance to their children is difficult in an environment they often do not all fully understand. Further, children become more secretive and private in their online actions as they get older. As they develop into adolescents, they demand privacy (and often a whole heap more) and share less and less. As they try to show themselves as mature and independent young people, they avoid sharing the negative aspects of their day, the unpleasant and sometimes spiteful comments that appear in their social media, and the sometimes-relentless pressure to share inappropriate images. Consider the following vignette about Sally.

When Sally enters a URL for a page she wants to visit into her web browser, a series of processes takes place. The school's filtering software compares the entered web address to those in its database. Inside the database is a regularly updated list of websites arranged into a series of broad categories. The school or district's network administrators set restrictions on which site categories are visible and which sites the system blocks. If the URL Sally entered is in a category of concern, it may even generate an alert.

Sally is aware that many of the sites she might visit are blocked and that if she uses a proxy server to anonymize her surfing to get around security measures, this can also flag an alert. Between the vigilance of the school's filtering system and the presence and awareness of her teacher, Sally has little opportunity to visit inappropriate sites.

It's a different story when Sally moves beyond the school's grounds and connects to Internet resources via her smartphone and, later, her home Wi-Fi. Sally's browsing activities then go unmonitored. Without the school's checks and filters, the entire Internet is but a couple of clicks away—the good, the bad, and the ugly.

Sally spends much of the evening connected to the home network and remains largely focused on the pressing demands of home learning and equally pressing social media likes and pokes. Like most of her peers, she switches inefficiently between tasks, listening to the latest tunes through the ever-present earbuds.

As the evening progresses, Sally receives a message from her boyfriend and, feigning tiredness, retires to her room with her phone. In the privacy of her room behind the closed door, the exchange continues. Encouraged by her boyfriend and safe in the fact that he would *never* share them, Sally uses Snapchat (an image messaging and multi-media mobile app) to capture revealing images of herself.

This vignette about Sally is fictional, but stories like this happen in homes and bedrooms across the planet. The restrictions and limitations enforced at school do not exist at home, nor do most families have the experience or skill to use products like OpenDNS (www.opendns.com), which allows category-based filtering in the home. Educators cannot control what goes on in students' homes, but in this chapter, we talk in detail about the guidance you can offer parents to make them your allies in developing students into good global digital citizens. We also talk about the responsibility schools face to work outside their walls to help students stay on the path.

Guidance for Parents

Parents of primary or elementary school students tend to come to every school meeting. They are passionately involved and interested in their children's progress, education, and development. This is partly because their children are dependent on them, and because younger children are eager to please their parents, seeking praise and reassurance.

Recall Erikson's stages of psychosocial development (n.d.) in table 5.1 (page 76). As young people mature into adolescents, they tend to withdraw from close parental contact. They become more private in their actions and behaviors, and have a drive for independence. Parents' attendance at meetings tends to drop as this happens, which is unfortunate given that this is precisely when students face ever-increasing social and emotional challenges, from cyberbullying to a growing awareness of their sexual identity. Therefore, it is critical that schools capture parent engagement early, not only as a means to maintain it later on but to make sure their perception of technology is not just of the dark side that news reports often sensationalize.

In this section, we cover the following topics.

- Parent engagement

- Anatomy of a parent meeting

- Apps to buy

- Digital citizenship guidelines for parents and education by ambush

- Accessible resources and materials

- Confidentiality

We start here, with parent engagement.

Parent Engagement

One way that many schools try to prevent dwindling parent involvement is by having regular parent information evenings on a range of topics, not the least of which is student technology use. The primary school in Andrew's district sponsors technology evenings called iPad 1.0, iPad 2.0, and so on; the school adds a digit for each new session. The sessions are for parents wanting to learn more about the devices the students are using to augment and transform their education and to seek answers for any concerns. These evenings are so well attended the school must run two to three of them per week to meet demand.

The evening sessions have a useful structure that school staff continually refine to better satisfy parents. The objectives of these sessions are as follows.

- Provide an overview of the purpose and significance of the technology program and device in their child's education.

- Build parent confidence with and use of the child's learning device.

- Establish an overview of technology use in the school.

- Give advice on device care and maintenance, including installation of apps and backup.

- Give advice on establishing appropriate use, setting restrictions, and connecting at home.

- Show the support mechanisms and processes the school has for parents.

- Provide an opportunity for question-and-answer sessions with key leaders.

Your own goals should reflect similar priorities, but ultimately, you must tailor them to fit the unique needs and priorities of your own school culture. With these priorities in mind, you can begin to establish an agenda.

Anatomy of a Parent Meeting

At Andrew's school, parents are asked to bring their child's device to use at information technology meetings. The parents are also asked to come alone; these sessions are for parents, not their children. School staff welcome the group and then explain the evening's agenda.

The room is set up with six to eight stations, each with a table facing a large flat-screen television. At these stations, pairs of responsible students demonstrate an activity they have recently done in class, while staff circulate and support the student-led presentations. The activities cover the range of curriculum areas. Staff encourage parents to access their child's device, open the specific apps, and engage in the activities.

This hands-on approach leads into an overview of the entire vision and objectives of the technology program. A school leader then concisely outlines the educational rationale behind the school's technology program, including its advantages. One of the things staff always stress as a key part of the program is the need for balance between screen time and device use, traditional classroom activities, and physical activity. Lee is often asked about striking a balance between home use of the device for schoolwork and for personal entertainment. We both believe that recreational screen time can't come at the expense of physical activity. If schoolwork, exercise, and chores are complete, personal entertainment is acceptable, but consider making it a social activity, something you do together. Do, however, keep in mind our recommendations that all devices stay in social areas, not in the bedrooms, and that family members turn off all devices, including televisions, two hours before bed.

Following this, a support team member runs through the device maintenance and backup. Since the parents have their child's device and Internet access at school, many take this opportunity to set up online backups. Staff also show parents how to set up restrictions and limitations on the device. It is important to note Andrew's school does not specify restrictions but offers support to the parents to establish their own appropriate set.

Staff then discuss cyber-safety, global digital citizenship, and appropriate use. This is an open discussion that lays bare many facts and misconceptions while detailing requirements for safe and appropriate use. Staff explain the school's digital citizenship agreements and classroom technology use, and then recommend what parents should do at home. They discuss access to app stores and game and media content ratings, as well as issues of copyright and piracy. A critical aspect of the evening is to explain the need for balance and supporting research about screen time, sleep, exercise, and play.

The underlying framework for providing parents with sound advice is what we call the three Is. The three Is of Internet safety, illustrated in table 6.1, are a quick snapshot of what parents need to support and protect their children.

Table 6.1: The Three Is of Internet Safety

Category	Description
Informed	Parents need a balanced perspective of technology use. It is important to present the positives and negatives. Technology is critical to learning and the future of our students, but parents are often only presented with a single side of the picture in the media. How good a device is for learning, and how engaging and relevant it is, do not grab viewer attention in the media, unlike the sometimes-tragic consequences of cyberbullying.
Interested	Parents are encouraged to be interested in their child's learning and technology use. They should be very familiar with it, look at their child's work, and have the child explain what they are doing, why they are doing it, and why it is significant. Being interested in their child's learning and online activities gives parents oversight of their child's activities and can lead to amazing discussions and quick identification of concerns, issues, or problems.
In view	Parents should keep devices out of bedrooms and in public spaces. Keeping all devices in view, while sometimes difficult, will help keep young people safe. It may involve the purchase of headphones to block out the noise of the games they are playing and will often involve chaos at the dining room table as the children spread out their stuff for home learning, but the advantages far outweigh the potential pitfalls.

These guidelines are applicable to students of every age, from primary or elementary school all the way through high school. Let's look more deeply at each of them.

1. **Informed:** Parents need a balanced perspective of technology use. The media's view of technology is often slanted toward sensationalism, grabbing headlines, and getting ratings. It is important to present parents with the risks, but not to neglect technology's benefits.

2. **Interested:** Parents are encouraged to be interested in their child's learning and technology use. Because teachers tell students what their learning outcomes are, getting them to explain the learning outcomes of the activity or task is very beneficial. The analogy we often use is to compare how their child's device is just like a traditional exercise book; parents flip through their child's book, read the teacher's comments, and ask the child what he or she is doing. The device is no different.

3. **In view:** We strongly recommend that devices stay out of bedrooms and remain in public spaces. Almost every cyber-safety agency across the planet echoes this advice. It is hard to surf pornography or access unacceptable material when the device is in the family room. It is hard to hide cyberbullying when the conversations are taking place in a shared space. It is almost impossible to be involved in sexting without a private space. In Andrew's home, there is a charging station and all devices (laptops, tablets, and phones) are placed on charge at the end of the evening. The stairs, which mark the boundary between the bedroom area of the house and the living areas, are the boundary for devices. Devices are not allowed upstairs or in bedrooms.

The final part of the parent meeting is a question-and-answer session, when parents ask a panel of senior leaders, support staff, and others any pressing questions or relay any concerns. Always be direct in answering parent concerns. Give parents honest answers and, when you cannot do so on the spot, offer to look more deeply at an issue and get back to them. Often the questions parents raise influence future information meetings or become part of the digital hints and suggestions offered in the school's newsletter.

Of course, keeping parents informed through informational meetings is only one way to maintain parent engagement at home. There are also the questions of what apps students are using, how teachers choose between the plethora of education apps available, and how to approach purchasing costs that affect parents.

Apps to Buy

The app stores for the various operating systems and devices present huge opportunities for educators. There are brilliant classroom applications that are sometimes free (although many have in-app purchases or upgrades for a fee) or only cost the equivalent of a few U.S. dollars. At the same time, parents will note any extra expense and it's important to have their buy-in for any app purchases you want them to make for their children.

A recommendation we often give parents is to ensure any purchases their child makes also require parents to log in to complete. Many device ecosystems (or product platforms) allow students to make app requests that notify parents and allow them to approve requests using their own devices. Students should not, under any circumstances, know their parents' app store passwords. We know a parent who left his app store access unlocked and available to his young charge only to later discover an $800 Visa bill.

With restrictions in place, parents see every application the school asks students to install on their devices. This, however, is not the only consideration when deciding on apps to use in the classroom. Parents often ask why a previous application was used and become frustrated if the teacher selected it on a whim and did not make full use of it in the classroom (or at all).

To help reduce parents' frustration, use a deliberate and considered approach to technology use and, at the end of the term, provide parents with a list of applications required for the following term. Schools should require teachers to test any applications they want to use within the school environment. Teachers should also integrate the applications' use into learning units. For apps that are not free, teachers should balance the applications' use with the cost and inconvenience of asking parents to purchase them. As with all technology, the questions teachers must consider are, How does this purchase help achieve a learning outcome? Is the benefit worth the investment? Consider these questions especially when apps offer free and paid versions. Free app versions are often missing critical features. Likewise, when a premium app version offers particularly valuable features that directly connect to learning outcomes, it's often worth the investment.

This process tends to be straightforward in early and even middle grades, when parents are generally actively engaged in their child's education. It gets trickier when their involvement erodes as students enter high school. Fortunately, there are ways to mitigate this problem.

Digital Citizenship Guidelines for Parents and Education by Ambush

The trend of decreasing parent involvement as their child ages means that providing suitable support to parents is increasingly difficult. To counteract this, Andrew and his primary school colleagues have adopted a new tactic for getting personal digital citizenship guidelines and other informative materials into parents' hands—*education by ambush*.

Whether it is parent apathy, student resistance, or perhaps the messages not reaching home, attendance by parents of older students at our safety sessions is very low. In Andrew's school, staff run three sessions to cater to demand, but the high school sessions rarely have more than three or four families attend. This does not mean, however, that there aren't opportunities to gain parent involvement. Some school events inevitably require full parent and student attendance. Most schools host a Meet the Teacher Night at the start of the school year (or some other form of welcome session), where parents bring students on a designated day to do course enrollments, device connections or pickups, and so on.

Andrew's school, for example, does a full planning week before school starts to address these prerequisite activities. This approach means that the first official week of school has an academic focus and sets the scene for the year. After an assembly in the first period of the day, classes begin. Students have their timetables, they are enrolled in the learning management system for their course selection, the class materials are available, and, from day one of the year, learning begins.

Global digital citizenship is not mentioned in any of the correspondence sent to parents but is a large component of the opening address to parents. Staff take an age-appropriate, balanced approach to providing relevant information to parents. Again, they explain the underlying principles of digital citizenship so the parents are aware of the school's guidelines and expectations. They also stress the importance of partnership, since the success of the technology program is based on the engagement of all three partners—the teachers, students, and parents. If one partner is not engaged, then chances of success are drastically reduced. As part of this partnership, the school distributes parent-applicable personal digital citizenship guidelines like those featured in figure 6.1 (page 90). (Appendix C, page 143, includes a reproducible version of this digital citizenship agreement.)

Digital Citizenship Personal Guidelines

Respect for myself by

- Showing respect for myself through my actions
- Considering what personal information about my life, experiences, experimentation, or relationships I post
- Considering the materials that I post online and how these may reflect on myself, my family, and the wider community, including my work
- Considering the sites that I visit and how they may reflect on me as a person and as a member of the family
- Not being obscene, degrading, rude, or inappropriate

Responsibility for myself by

- Considering the impact of my actions and behaviors and consequences of my actions on myself and my family
- Being balanced in my use of technology and being informed and aware of both the risks and benefits of my technology use
- Separating my personal and professional use of technology
- Protecting my identity; ensuring that the information, images, and materials I post online will not put me or my family at risk
- Considering the personal information I have published and the social networks that I have joined; being aware that the audience may be broader and wider than I intended
- Taking suitable steps to ensure my online and offline safety and privacy
- Taking steps to protect my data
- Reporting any attacks or inappropriate behavior directed at me and seeking support from appropriate people or organizations
- Protecting passwords, bank and credit card accounts, and resources

Respect for others by

- Using appropriate language and judgment when sending emails, posts, or messages— even when angry
- Selecting appropriate mediums and social networks for my personal communications, showing consideration to others, and understanding the limitations of the mediums
- Not using electronic mediums to flame, bully, harass, or stalk other people
- Being conscientious in my choice of websites; avoiding, whenever possible, visiting sites that are inappropriate, degrading, pornographic, or racist
- Not abusing my rights of access
- Being a role model for appropriate use of technology

Responsibility for others by

- Guiding, educating, and supporting my family and friends in the appropriate use of technology

- Modeling balanced use of technologies; setting an example of restraint, appropriate use, balance, and respect

- Being intolerant of abuse whether directed at or stemming from my family and friends; taking appropriate steps to deal with such, including reporting abuse

- Balancing the often-conflicting needs for safety and privacy in our use of technology

- Taking appropriate steps to ensure the safety and privacy of my family and friends; seeking permission beforehand to post their personal information, photos, videos, and so on

- Limiting access to information to those who should have access to it; considering the privacy settings and groups that material is published to

- Moderating unacceptable materials and conversations; reporting conversations that are inappropriate or unacceptable

- Not forwarding inappropriate materials or communications

Respect for property by

- Modeling appropriate purchasing of software and media; being intolerant of piracy of materials including music, movies, and other media by my family and friends

- Requesting permission to use resources; respecting and abiding by copyright, intellectual property, and patent

- Validating information and checking the accuracy of advisory posts and emails I receive

- Guiding and supporting my family and friends

Responsibility for property by

- Being aware of my legal rights in regard to using copyrighted media; understanding my rights for backup and distribution of different media within my immediate family

- Suitably protecting other people's rights to protect their copyright and intellectual property

- Using only appropriately obtained, licensed, and registered software and media

- Suitably protecting our systems to ensure their security and integrity

- Reporting vandalism and damage

By signing this agreement, I undertake to always act in a manner that is respectful to myself and others, and to act appropriately, and in a moral and ethical manner.

I, _____, agree to follow the principles of digital citizenship outlined in this agreement and accept that failing to follow these tenets will have consequences.

Signed: _____

Date: _____ / _____ / _____

Figure 6.1: Digital citizenship—personal guidelines.

Even if there isn't full parent involvement in school activities, it's still important to ensure information resources, including personal digital citizenship guidelines, are available online, so parents who do not attend these events still have access to them.

Accessible Resources and Materials

The school's website is a great place to host the relevant materials. A section dedicated to acceptable use and global digital citizenship is a great asset for parents. Ideally, the section contains at least some of the following.

- The rationale and vision for global digital citizenship

- The use agreements and guidelines for students, staff, and parents

- Links to relevant and supportive national and international resources for students

- A clear and concise pathway for parent and student support

- Helpful hints and recommendations for maximizing device use

Like all sections of school websites, this section should be easily accessible and not buried behind a long sequence of clicks and menus. Of course, making parents aware of this information does not necessarily get their buy-in, especially if they fear any poor citizenship choices their child makes will have humiliating consequences.

Confidentiality

Unfortunately, experience shows us that sometimes inappropriate and often dangerous actions and behaviors go unreported because both parents and students have concerns about being identified. Some parents, faced with confronting their increasingly independent and sometimes resistant child, avoid the angst and conflict that come with consequences for poor choices; in other words, they allow behaviors and actions that are dangerous to either their child or others to slip past them. Ensuring confidentiality and providing a safe and secure mechanism for reporting concerns enable and facilitate these critical conversations. Many schools we've worked with have adopted systems where anonymous sources can submit a report. During a program's early stages, this can be helpful, but as understanding grows over time, this becomes less necessary as both parents and students feel the importance of taking action.

The confidentiality this system provides can also be helpful for students that face issues at home. In previous chapters, we've discussed consequences for not living up to standards in a digital citizenship agreement. Students face consequences from teachers and parents for not living up to its terms. Teachers can face professional consequences. What consequences exist for parents and the wider community that can help get their buy-in? This is a very challenging issue as there are few enforceable consequences for parents given that most are beyond the school's control. However, if parent behavior becomes a safety issue affecting the student, a reporting system such as this can be a real asset.

These issues are not the only ones that schools face. Indeed, knowing when to draw borders between private parenting choices and student behavior that affects the school and other students is challenging. Knowing where school involvement should start and finish requires careful forethought.

School Responsibility

A school's responsibility, or perhaps influence, extends well beyond its grounds and hours of active instruction. Engaging the wider community involves making connections outside the school beyond engaging parents. Accomplishing this requires making a choice between taking the easy route or the hard route to maintain active involvement in students' development. It also involves developing a shared vision between schools and understanding what constitutes a harmful digital communication.

The Easy Route

It is easy for a school to just fulfill its basic responsibility for reasonable care of students. A school can simply focus only on providing a safe learning environment within the time they are *in loco parentis* (in place of a parent). That is to say, educators have a legal responsibility to take on some of the functions and responsibilities of a parent while the student is in school ("In loco parentis," n.d.). This often involves a basic whitelist or blacklist approach to Internet access, a sequence of restrictions and rules for behavior, and bare-minimum follow-up consequences for infractions.

Going the *easy route* means providing instruction that meets only the requirements of the state or nationally required curricula. Taking your school beyond these minimum requirements may require effort from faculty, students, and parents, but it generates greater results.

The Hard Route

Most school mission statements include the catchphrase, *lifelong learners*. Even though much of the digital knowledge students acquire now will be obsolete by the time they graduate or continue their education, the skills, attributes, and attitudes teachers instill in them remain for a lifetime.

The *hard route* means working with the communities beyond the school day and school grounds. By accepting that the school is a linchpin for the lives of young people, and that educators' influence and sphere of responsibility go beyond the limitations of the traditional vision of the school, you can provide a holistic and beneficial education for your students.

Working in partnership with students and parents means that education does not stop at the school's door. Looking specifically at global digital citizenship, if all partners know the expectations and their roles, then it is easier for all to fulfill them. This partnership entails the following.

- Clear and realistic expectations

- Open and accessible lines of communication

- Clear understanding of rationale and consequences

- Suitable support mechanisms

The student who is being cyberbullied while at home should be able to seek and receive support at school. The impact of incidents beyond the school has a huge effect on the student's learning and his or her interactions with peers and teachers. Cyberbullying affects the student's motivation and enthusiasm to learn, participate, contribute, and thrive (StopBullying.gov, n.d.).

The reality is nothing is separate. Students cannot partition their lives into silos any more than educators can. It makes sense to teach skills you know are valuable at and beyond school with a suitable, shared approach. That approach does not just establish connections between school and home but also between other schools.

Shared Vision Between Schools

In what is an all-too-common occurrence, imagine a student at one school harassing a student at another school. We witnessed one such example in which the harassment took the form of setting up a profile on the popular dating app, Tinder. This profile implied that the young person was interested in a range of deviant activities. The profile used images of the young person without permission and was grossly offensive. The spiteful and malicious actions of the bully mortified and hurt the victim.

Although Tinder quickly removed the profile after the family contacted them, by this stage the damage was already done. The school in question did contact the school the offending student attended, but it was never clear whether it took actions to prevent this from happening again.

For this reason, among many others, establishing a network of schools across the city or district with a shared basis for global digital citizenship, and then building a memorandum of understanding containing protocols and procedures for dealing with such incidents, is a benefit to all. Such a memorandum of understanding should cover at least the following.

- A contact person for each school

- The investigation process for alleged incidents

- The potential consequences of proven activities

- Outcomes reported back to the originating school

- Restorative justice and closure for the victim

- Humanization of the activities to show the significance of the impact on the victim

- The threshold for reporting to judicial authorities

For the victim, this type of memorandum allows for resolution; for the bully, it enables humanization. It is too easy, from the safety of the keyboard and screen, to shield bullies from ever witnessing the effects of their actions. Such a network and memorandum can open the bullies' eyes to the human cost of their actions. The unified support from schools also goes a long way to ensure that students understand that inappropriate actions and behaviors that lead to potentially harmful digital communications are dealt with appropriately and consistently across all schools.

Unsurprisingly, determining what consequences are or are not appropriate varies from region to region. What works for some cultures may not make sense for others. This is why we offer frameworks for sound methodology, but not strict models. If your school's practice is to suspend students for theft, it should also suspend them for downloading pirated software. The important points are not just what you do, but that what you do is consistent, fair, and in adherence with your community's values. Part of this process also includes differentiating between what is and isn't harmful.

Harmful Digital Communications

A difficulty many schools experience in determining when they have a responsibility to get involved is that sometimes it is hard to describe what constitutes a harmful digital communication. Without guidance, it can be hard to develop an understanding of the complexity and seriousness of the actions. Several countries have created legislation regarding such communications. In New Zealand, the Harmful Digital Communications Act 2015 provides a useful framework to help build definitions and other frameworks.

The framework is a series of ten principles that define what acceptable digital communications should be:

> Principle 1: A digital communication should not disclose sensitive personal facts about an individual.

> Principle 2: A digital communication should not be threatening, intimidating, or menacing.

> Principle 3: A digital communication should not be grossly offensive to a reasonable person in the position of the affected individual.

Principle 4: A digital communication should not be indecent or obscene.

Principle 5: A digital communication should not be used to harass an individual.

Principle 6: A digital communication should not make a false allegation.

Principle 7: A digital communication should not contain a matter that is published in breach of confidence.

Principle 8: A digital communication should not incite or encourage anyone to send a message to an individual for the purpose of causing harm to the individual.

Principle 9: A digital communication should not incite or encourage an individual to commit suicide.

Principle 10: A digital communication should not denigrate an individual by reason of his or her colour, race, ethnic or national origins, religion, gender, sexual orientation, or disability. (Harmful Digital Communications Act 2015, section 6, pp. 5–6)

Perhaps in recognition of the key role of education, the New Zealand act also empowers principals or their delegates to bring proceedings to the district courts: "The professional leader of a registered school or his or her delegate, if the affected individual is a student of that school and consents to the professional leader or delegate bringing the proceedings" (Harmful Digital Communications Act 2015, section 11, p. 9).

Schools can adapt and use such clear principles as they provide a basis for what is and isn't acceptable.

Of course, schools, parents, and the community can only do so much. There are times when legal recourse is the only suitable pathway. When the actions of an individual endanger others or place the individual at risk of self-harm, then the only course is through legal avenues. At this point, clearly defined and implemented processes of investigation and evidence gathering, and clear and appropriate school policies, are critical.

Beyond the Wider Community

In this chapter, we discussed growing the wider community, which is by far the most challenging aspect of establishing digital citizenship practices. This is largely because parents, unlike teachers and students, are not in the school all day and holding them accountable is very difficult, sometimes impossible. The best way to ensure their involvement is with relevance and a strong personal connection. They need to feel and believe in the program. This is an important step to creating global digital citizens, because as we explore in the next chapter, this is the real purpose of this initiative. What happens in our digital lives transfers to the physical world and has the potential for creating significant global change.

Guiding Questions

As you reflect on this chapter, consider the following six guiding questions.

1. Why do parents need support and guidance on global digital citizenship like students and staff?

2. Why does parent involvement tend to lessen as students mature?

3. Parents are often only exposed to the seedier side of global digital citizenship and technology use through the media. How can you act at the school level to change parent perceptions?

4. What are the three Is, and what role do they play in parent support?

5. Why is it crucial that the school's role include support for both parents and students in all aspects of their digital lives?

6. What should happen in cases where actions and behaviors are so severe that the school cannot deal with them?

Growing Global Digital Citizenship

Global digital citizenship is more than simply reading agreements, following guidelines, and adopting mindsets. It's a way of living and a living process. It's a seed we plant in our minds that steadily grows into a set of unconscious beliefs and practices that will one day transform the entire world.

Like any living seeds, the ideas of global digital citizenship are better nurtured with time in a rich and fertile environment. They need a little feeding and tending to every day. Awareness, practice, and open discussion help keep these ideas alive and growing.

In this chapter, we examine the value of teachable moments and how the daily act of teaching offers spontaneous moments to stress the tenets of good global digital citizenship. Looking broader, we examine two schools that embrace these tenets and reap the rewards. And we present a series of learning projects you can use in your classroom to get students thinking about and practicing global digital citizenship.

Teachable Moments

Teachable moments are everywhere, and you can use them with your students to continue fostering global digital citizenship. For example, there's a story about a teacher who happened to be instructing his students in the courteous art of silencing their smartphones before class (and in many other public venues) when his own phone went off in the middle of the lecture. Having one of the more obnoxious downloadable ringtones available made the situation even more hilarious!

Of course, the class roared with laughter, forcing a choice on the teacher. He could have been defensive and dismissive of his own mistake or embrace it. In the end, he decided to gladly make himself both the brunt of the joke and the focus of the lesson, citing the embarrassment he was feeling as one of the many incentives for practicing cell phone courtesy. This led him to embrace critical teaching questions such as,

"My phone has just taken everyone off task and interrupted the learning. Am I being responsible for myself? Am I respecting others?" In the end, everyone learned something and had fun doing it. That's the instructional power of a teachable moment. An acceptable use policy is signed for compliance and filed in a drawer, but global digital citizenship is a living program that the school and wider community constantly refer to and debate.

However, global digital citizenship doesn't thrive on teachable moments alone; it must become part of the culture and pedagogy. Only then does it become a living process, which means it will grow in the hearts and minds of the students, teachers, and the wider community. Let's look at two such schools that ingrained global digital citizenship into an everyday aspect of their cultures.

Melrose Embraces Essential Fluencies

As preparation for the ACT assessment, Melrose High School in Canberra, Australia, has been using the essential fluencies for several years. Students at Melrose have longstanding direct exchanges with schools in Japan and Taiwan. These hosted home-stay opportunities help build a deep understanding of living in another culture and assist in building connections to others in the world. By developing international relationships and sharing ideas, schools can personalize and share the global issues that face each student.

In addition to this physical-global connection, Melrose students altruistically have led younger students in a solution fluency challenge. For example, high school students mentored fifth-grade students through solution fluency to create and pitch solutions to global issues. The younger students generated issues that concerned them related to global conflict, world hunger, global warming, and terrorism. One team of students worked through their global issue on conflict by designing a global currency that would eliminate economic inequities, which they believed to be the cause of conflict. Not bad at eleven years old!

Because they embrace fluencies in this way, students at Melrose have a deep tradition of altruistic service and a focus on environmental stewardship, and they fully embrace digital citizenship behaviors. The school uses the global digital citizenship program to build the global digital citizens of the future—students who have a deep sense of personal responsibility for finding solutions to today's issues.

De La Salle Embraces Global Matters

In another example, De La Salle College Ashfield in Australia (a secondary day school for boys) became engaged with a global digital citizen program because it allows students to further deepen their understanding of how the world works. This helps them tap into the notion of developing personal responsibility and fostering positive relationships. The school embraced the idea that all students have a choice to make in determining how they develop a level of personal responsibility within the global environment.

The school used digital citizenship agreements to complement its existing principles of respect, which forms positive relationships. The boys easily identify notions of respect for oneself, others, and property, which encouraged them to consider their actions with empathy and respect while acknowledging the global connectedness of society.

The school's embrace of teachable moments allows staff and students to discuss real-world issues saturated in the media. This opened the door for critical thinking and deep classroom discussion, something that often brought more questions, which then became further challenges for the boys. We found it heartening to see the boys adopt a glass-half-full approach to their learning and conversations. Furthermore, staff often use the teachable moments as opportunities to enrich the curriculum and promote professional discussion.

Many schools have echoed the successes at Melrose and De La Salle. To assist you and your school, the following section details some of the scenarios and global matters used at these schools. There are many more to be found on the Global Digital Citizen Foundation website (https://globaldigitalcitizen.org).

Global Digital Citizenship Project-Based Learning Scenarios

In your quest to help grow your students into global digital citizens, use these project-based learning scenarios to help sow and grow the seeds of global digital citizenship. These short scenario ideas for lessons foster global digital citizenship awareness. These ideas come from our solution fluency activity planner, something we cover in depth in *Mindful Assessment* (Crockett & Churches, 2017). You can find many more at the Global Digital Citizenship Foundation (www.solutionfluency.com), where you can sign up and begin building your own lessons and collaborating with teachers all over the world. (This planner includes free and pay-for subscriptions.)

A Changing World (Primary School)

Essential question: What do you consider to be the most important factors for humans and animals to coexist in a changing environment?

Subjects: Science, economics, geography

Scenario: A few members of your town have wondered where the displaced animals and birds will go when the area is leveled and the shrubbery around the lake is removed to make a man-made beach. They are concerned that the creatures may end up in town. Because they are not suited to live there, many will die or become nuisances. Your class has been asked to evaluate this issue and discover how the proposed beach will affect the local wildlife. You all have been asked to research the animals that live in the affected area (in the lake, on the shores of the lake, or in the lightly forested region near the lake).

Your class will make a presentation at the next town council meeting to share what you learned from your research. Your slideshow presentation will need to include three animals or plants that live in the area from a list. For each of these, list one of the ways that animals affect the environment and how that is relevant to the beach project. For each animal, explain how the beach project is likely to affect the animal. Will that animal be able to cope on a well-used public beach, or will they be displaced?

Gratitude Group (Primary School)

Essential question: How could you use a public event to create awareness and express your appreciation of the people in your community?

Subjects: Language arts, social studies, mathematics

Scenario: Take a moment and think about the people who work to make the community strong through the services they provide to its economy. What would you come up with if you had one day to create a celebration to show these people how much you and your community appreciate them? Create a unique community celebration showing appreciation for your community leaders and their day-to-day efforts. Use research about expressing thanks in cultures around the world, and make something to show your community how much it matters!

Welcome, World! (Middle School)

Essential question: What common interests can students of different cultures share with each other using images and stories?

Subjects: Language arts, social studies, art, design

Scenario: Pictures can convey so many feelings and emotions, and you can also use them to share feelings about important points in your life or others' lives. Your school is going to incorporate a new student exchange program, and you've got a great idea. You're going to provide a promotional package for overseas students. Create an online photo book to send to schools in different countries. Share details about what it's like to live and learn where you are from. With visuals and text, present your community and your school in a way that would help your reader to understand what makes your school and community unique or interesting. Capture exciting events or class projects and detail them in a photo book to turn it into an adventure.

Radical Recyclers (Middle School)

Essential question: How can recycling help you with your own fundraising?

Subjects: Mathematics, economics, design, language arts

Scenario: Recycling events are a popular fundraising strategy for schools and other organizations. People donate recyclable items, from aluminum cans to computer components, and the money from recycling goes to the group that sponsors the recycling event. A group of students at your school would like to organize a recycling fundraiser, but they need to convince your school principal that the project will be profitable. Use your mathematics skills to create scenarios for three different recyclable items, giving detailed calculations in the form of linear functions to make your case!

Green Gears (High School)

Essential question: How can you use waste products to counteract the effects of consuming conventional fuel sources?

Subjects: Science, mathematics, design, environmental studies, technology

Scenario: Picture a future where alternative fuel sources remedy many of our environmental issues, such as waste and recycling. With a little ingenuity and some extensive research and experimentation, you can create a solution to benefit all. Come up with your own machine that runs on an alternative fuel source. Work in groups and research the innovations in this field as inspiration for your own designs. How will your creation work, and how will it serve humanity?

The Greenway (High School)

Essential question: How do greenways and green transportation routes improve the quality of the environment in large cities?

Subjects: Social studies, design, urban planning, technology, sustainability, digital technology

Scenario: It's time for you to start thinking green! Work in groups to design and present ideas for a green transportation corridor in your city. Become inspired by actual urban-planning procedures and follow examples of eco-friendly initiatives other cities have put in place. As a team, research a suitable transportation corridor or other location that could accommodate a pedestrian walkway, bicycle lane, or commuter trail or pathway. Design the walkway or bicycle lane with aesthetics in mind, and make sure it is wide enough to accommodate two directions of traffic. Use natural elements such as grass, trees, or other foliage to make your greenway something your city can be proud of.

Resources for Maintaining Global Digital Citizenship Mindsets

Cultivating global digital citizenship mindsets in students remains an ongoing process. We want to make sure you have all the tools you need to keep it in your students' hearts and minds. In the three appendices (pages 107–154), we include additional tools to help you foster and grow global digital citizenship in your teaching and learning endeavors. Here is a brief description of each tool.

1. **Global Matters (appendix A, page 107):** Use these engaging discussion sessions on global events and issues to engage your students to think as global citizens. Discuss the articles, view the videos, and then create class interactions about the topic using the provided questions. Visit **go.SolutionTree.com/technology** to download free copies of these mindful moment discussions.

2. **Activity Sheets (appendix B, page 133):** Each of these reproducible activity sheets relates to the use agreement guidelines for primary, middle, and high schools. The sheets are meant to stir ideas and debates that foster an understanding about the agreement ideals. Visit the Global Digital Citizen Foundation (https://globaldigitalcitizen.org) or **go.SolutionTree.com /technology** to download free copies of these activities.

3. **Digital Citizenship Agreements (appendix C, page 143):** This appendix includes not only the digital citizenship agreements from chapter 3 but also professional and personal digital citizenship guidelines found in chapters 4 and 6. Visit **go.SolutionTree.com/technology** to download free copies of these guidelines.

With this book and these tools, you have what you need to drive your students forward on the path to being good global digital citizens.

Next Steps

As technology and connectivity continue to shape our lives in every conceivable way, we will continue to see the idea of what it means to be a good global digital citizen evolve, as well as the influence that global digital citizens have on the world. When it comes to maintaining the mindfulness of such citizenship, the keys are diligence and a healthy dose of patience. Global digital citizenship and its disciplines are like any other skill worth learning—they take time to master. Once that happens, their unconscious presence becomes a way of life. That's when the world really begins to change.

We hope this book has taught you a lot about global digital citizens—who they are and what they stand for. We've provided some great tools to help you understand and implement these values in your teaching practices.

We strongly believe that we can overcome many of the challenges we face by investing in our youth. Children are a small percentage of our population, but they are 100 percent of our future. Growing global digital citizens is about creating a generation of caring, compassionate, responsible, and ethical young people with the tools and capacity to shape and share this world to create a bright future for all beings.

Change, however, requires action. It starts right now, with you.

No matter who you are, where you are, or what you do, you can begin taking small steps toward building solid foundations for global digital citizenship tenets and attitudes in both yourself and students.

Perhaps you are a parent with an eye on social media and its benefits and perils. Maybe you're a teacher who wants to know how best to harness the responsible use of connectivity in your classroom and school culture. You could be an IT enthusiast or businessperson with an interest in watching how the latest technological trends will affect how you work and communicate with people across the office or around the globe. Or you could be all of these things. We recommend that you begin your journey using the three crucial guiding questions for this chapter.

Guiding Questions

As you reflect on this chapter, consider the following three guiding questions.

1. What are three things you didn't know before that you know now?

2. What are two questions that have come to mind while reading this book that you intend to find the answers to?

3. What's the one action that you're going to start taking right now?

Appendix A
Global Matters

Addressing global events and issues with your students is the basis for the discussion sessions we include in this appendix. You can discuss with students the articles, have them view the videos, and then create class interactions about the topic using the provided questions. This appendix also includes frameworks for quick student assessment. Visit **go.SolutionTree.com/technology** to download free copies. Note that you can find original versions of each of these global matters on our Global Digital Citizen Foundation website (https://globaldigitalcitizen.org).

China's Growing Consumer Waste Challenge

The consumer waste problem in China is a growing one. But just how bad is it, and what can we expect to see happen?

As China's economy shifts, William Morris (2015) writes that by 2025 the country's urban consumer population will expand by about three hundred million. As China more frequently uses white goods, consumables, and electronics, consumer waste is expected to multiply.

Morris also reports that China produces an estimated 28 percent of the plastic waste in our oceans, and about $32 billion in food waste annually. Most of this food waste ends up in landfills, which produce methane that poisons nearby lands and farms. Thus, farmers counter this problem with heavy fertilizer application that ultimately destroys the natural nutrient balance of workable soil.

In the end, the picture is grim. As China's population increases, so will its levels of consumer waste. It's only a matter of time before the issue becomes too dangerous to ignore. China must act aggressively against waste accumulation before this is allowed to happen.

More Resources

Use the following resources to conduct your research.

- **"China's Trash Is Taking Over" (Vanderklippe, 2015):** *www.theglobeandmail.com/news/world/chinas-trash-is-taking-over/article24367032*

- **"China's Electronic Waste Village" (Getty, n.d.):** *http://content.time.com/time/photogallery/0,29307,1870162,00.html*

- **"Ways Forward From China's Urban Waste Problem" (Li, 2015):** *https://thenatureofcities.com/2015/02/01/ways-forward-from-chinas-urban-waste-problem*

- **"China's Rural Dumping Grounds" (Eisenstark, 2015):** *www.slate.com/articles/life/caixin/2015/05/china_s_waste_management_garbage_disposal_in_the_country_s_rural_areas_is.html*

- **"Trash or Treasure? Prospects for China's Recycling Industry" (US-China Business Council, 2016):** *www.chinabusinessreview.com/trash-or-treasure-prospects-for-chinas-recycling-industry*

Discussion Questions

Use the following questions to facilitate your classroom discussion.

- *How does one nation's waste management (or mismanagement) affect its neighboring nations?*

- *What are the physical, emotional, and psychological effects of living in an environment where waste buildup is a concern?*

- *How do you manage your own personal consumer waste, and what could you do better?*

- *Why are we less concerned with waste and littering than we should be, even though we know it's a problem that affects the world?*

- *If left unchecked, what do you predict would be the national and global impact of a growing waste problem in China in 2025? 2030?*

- *Great things often begin with small actions. What actions could China's citizens take to better manage waste on a personal level?*

Global Digital Citizen Assessment Framework

Use this four-phase assessment framework to establish the connection between environmental stewardship and stimulating global awareness and action.

1. **Phase 1 (awareness, connection, remembering):** Has an awareness of some of the environmental issues and, when encouraged, may participate in activities to reduce this or raise awareness of them

2. **Phase 2 (understanding, applying):** Has an interest in and understanding of some environmental issues; supports local environmental activities, sometimes taking a stand on significant issues

3. **Phase 3 (analyzing, evaluating):** Shows an interest in global environmental issues and investigates causes or concerns before offering support; often takes a stand on current matters, undertaking appropriate actions that raise awareness; sometimes shows stewardship of his or her world

4. **Phase 4 (evaluating, creating):** Shows an active interest in global environmental issues; validates causes or concerns before offering support; takes a stand on matters of importance, undertaking appropriate actions that raise awareness of concerns through legitimate and appropriate means; shows stewardship, care, and responsibility for his or her world; thinks globally while acting locally

Discussion and Assessment Debrief

After conversation, students develop their own opinions about the assessment.

- *How did you evaluate this line from the assessment framework and why?*

- *How does the line from the assessment framework fit into the conversation?*

- *What does it mean for us? For the community? For the world?*

References

Eisenstark, R. (2015, May 29). China's rural dumping grounds. *Slate*. Accessed at www.slate.com/articles/life/caixin/2015/05/china_s_waste_management _garbage_disposal_in_the_country_s_rural_areas_is.html on January 16, 2017.

Getty. (n.d.). China's electronic waste village. *Time*. Accessed at http://content .time.com/time/photogallery/0,29307,1870162,00.html on January 16, 2017.

Li, J. (2015, February 1). *Ways forward from China's urban waste problem*. Accessed at https://thenatureofcities.com/2015/02/01/ways-forward -from-chinas-urban-waste-problem on January 16, 2017.

Morris, W. (2015, November 2). *China's growing consumer waste challenge*. Accessed at www.coresponsibility.com/china-and-consumer-waste on January 16, 2017.

US-China Business Council. (2016, April 6). *Trash or treasure? Prospects for China's recycling industry*. Accessed at www.chinabusinessreview.com /trash-or-treasure-prospects-for-chinas-recycling-industry on January 16, 2017.

Vanderklippe, N. (2015, May 11). China's trash is taking over. *Globe and Mail*. Accessed at www.theglobeandmail.com/news/world/chinas-trash-is -taking-over/article24367032 on January 16, 2017.

The True Cost of Digital Piracy

This topic provides a breakdown of how commonly practiced digital piracy hurts some industries. Many pirates think that theirs is a victimless crime. According to Joanne Seiff (2016), a published author, this is far from the truth.

Seiff (2016) begins by explaining that most artists and writers are unable to support themselves with their work royalty payments. In a particularly sobering moment in the article, she goes on to clarify just how her publishers calculate costs and royalties and how her books' earnings failed to outearn her advances, resulting in her earning no royalties from her publisher. (She is a seven-year veteran of publishing, with two books to her credit.) With her publisher's blessing, she digitally republished some of her content online, earning a mere $500 for her troubles. The reason she didn't earn more? Almost immediately after her content entered the digital space, it showed up on dozens of websites that illegally make such content freely available for download.

Digital piracy of this sort means that a copy of an artist's work can be downloaded and passed on literally thousands of times, with only a one-time payment going to the artist. That means that digital piracy does something far more harmful than cost artists money—it robs creative ideas of their value.

More Resources

Use the following resources to conduct your research.

- **"Is the Streaming Industry Lying About Piracy?" (Hassan, 2016):** *www .digitalmusicnews.com/2016/03/31/is-streaming-making-piracy-worse*

- **"The War on Internet Piracy" (Molla & Ovide, 2016):** *www.bloomberg.com /gadfly/articles/2016-03-23/google-and-media-titans-clash-in-a-war-on -internet-piracy*

- **"No Big Deal? Copyright and Piracy Online" (Vitrium, 2014):** *www.vitrium .com/media/images/no-big-deal-copyright-piracy-online.jpg*

- **"Top 10 Most Common Digital Piracy Myths Busted: Who's Pirating What and Why?" (Lanaria, 2016):** *www.techtimes.com/articles/121118/20160105 /top-10-most-common-digital-piracy-myths-busted-who-s-pirating-what -and-why.htm*

Discussion Questions

Use the following questions to facilitate your classroom discussion.

- *Do you agree or disagree with digital piracy? Why?*

- *What are some of the hidden costs of Internet piracy (psychological, emotional, and so on)?*

page 1 of 3

- *Put yourself in the role of an artist whose work has been pirated and shared illegally. What is your personal reaction or response?*

- *Do you believe digital piracy will get better or worse as time goes on? Why?*

- *Which do you feel is a more effective deterrent against digital piracy and why: stricter laws or evasion strategies?*

- *Do you think industry labels and companies could be doing more to help artists suffering from the effects of digital piracy? What could they do?*

Global Digital Citizen Assessment Framework

Use this four-phase assessment framework to establish the connection between digital citizenship and respect and responsibility for property.

1. **Phase 1 (awareness, connection, remembering):** Has an awareness of the laws of copyright, intellectual property, and privacy; occasionally cites sources in a suitable manner

2. **Phase 2 (understanding, applying):** Can follow the guidelines and norms for digital property; shows an understanding of the laws surrounding copyright, intellectual property, and privacy and sometimes applies them; occasionally requests permission to use resources and suitably cites sources

3. **Phase 3 (analyzing, evaluating):** Is often thoughtful in his or her online actions; shows a general understanding of the laws surrounding copyright, intellectual property, and privacy and often applies them; sometimes requests permission to use property, acknowledges ownership, and cites resources

4. **Phase 4 (evaluating, creating):** Shows consistent deliberation and consideration in his or her online actions; possesses a deep and rich understanding of the laws surrounding copyright, intellectual property, and privacy and applies them ethically; requests permission to use property and abides by the owners' rights to deny use; is always respectful and responsible in acknowledging ownership, citing resources, and protecting and securing sites and data; is considerate and reciprocal in others' requests to use his or her intellectual property

Discussion and Assessment Debrief

After conversation, students develop their own opinions about the assessment.

- *How did you evaluate this line from the assessment framework and why?*

- *How does the line from the assessment framework fit into the conversation?*

- *What does it mean for us? For the community? For the world?*

References

Hassan, C. (2016, March 31). Is the streaming industry lying about piracy? *Digital Music News*. Accessed at www.digitalmusicnews.com/2016/03/31/is -streaming-making-piracy-worse on January 16, 2017.

Lanaria, V. (2016, January 5). *Top 10 most common digital piracy myths busted: Who's pirating what and why?* Accessed at www.techtimes.com /articles/121118/20160105/top-10-most-common-digital-piracy-myths -busted-who-s-pirating-what-and-why.htm on January 16, 2017.

Molla, R., & Ovide, S. (2016, March 23). *The war on Internet piracy*. Accessed at www.bloomberg.com/gadfly/articles/2016-03-23/google-and-media -titans-clash-in-a-war-on-internet-piracy on January 16, 2017.

Seiff, J. (2016, March 13). *Time to assess the true cost of digital piracy, says Winnipeg author*. Accessed at www.cbc.ca/news/canada/manitoba/time -to-reconsider-the-cost-digital-piracy-1.3488270 on January 16, 2017.

Vitrium. (2014). *No big deal? Copyright and piracy online* [Infographic]. Accessed at www.vitrium.com/media/images/no-big-deal-copyright-piracy-online .jpg on January 16, 2017.

Inside the World's Biggest E-Waste Dump

This is a discussion of the (former) Agbogbloshie wetland on the outskirts of Accra in Ghana. It's an illegal e-waste dumping ground where outdated technology from the West is dumped and left to poison the land, air, and people. Those who work in this area salvage parts for what amounts to only dollars a day. In many cases, students who should be in school are working in Agbogbloshie.

Environmental concerns include fluorocarbon emissions, as well as lead, mercury, and hydrogen cyanide seeping into the soil in and around the dumping ground. Many of the workers admit to using marijuana as a deterrent to the headaches and chest pains they experience due to the toxicity of the environment.

In 2014, the organization Pure Earth opened a recycling center in Agbogbloshie to combat the adverse effects on the environment and the health of its people.

More Resources

Use the following resources to conduct your research.

- *"Agbogbloshie: The World's Largest E-Waste Dump—in Pictures" (McElvaney, 2014):* www.theguardian.com/environment/gallery/2014/feb/27 /agbogbloshie-worlds-largest-e-waste-dump-in-pictures

- *"(UPDATE) Transforming Agbogbloshie: From Toxic Dump Into Model Recycling Center" (Sim, 2015):* www.pureearth.org/blog/photos -transforming-agbogbloshie-from-toxic-e-waste-dump-into-model -recycling-center

- *"Anatomy of a Myth: The World's Biggest E-Waste Dump Isn't" (Minter, 2015):* http://shanghaiscrap.com/2015/06/anatomy-of-a-myth-the-worlds -biggest-e-waste-dump-isnt

- *"Ghana: Digital Dumping Ground" (Frontline/World, 2009):* www.pbs.org /frontlineworld/stories/ghana804/video/video_index.html

Discussion Questions

Use the following questions to facilitate your classroom discussion.

- *Where do you think this problem began? How far back can we trace the origin point?*

- *Having an idea where it started, what do you think could have been done to avoid it?*

- *Why do you think it is we allow things like this to continue happening?*

- *Imagine having a dumping ground like this in your city. How would it affect your life and the lives of those in your community?*

- *Where else in the world is this happening, and what is being done to stop it?*

- *Who has tried to solve this problem so far, and what have they done?*

- *What could Agbogbloshie do differently to help the environment and the people working there?*

- *What affirmative action would you take to help solve this problem?*

Global Digital Citizen Assessment Framework

Use this four-phase assessment framework to establish the connection between environmental stewardship and global awareness and action.

1. **Phase 1 (awareness, connection, remembering):** Has an awareness of some of the environmental issues and, when encouraged, may participate in activities to reduce this or raise awareness of them

2. **Phase 2 (understanding, applying):** Has an interest in and understanding of some environmental issues; supports local environmental activities, sometimes taking a stand on significant issues

3. **Phase 3 (analyzing, evaluating):** Shows an interest in global environmental issues and investigates causes or concerns before offering support; often takes a stand on current matters, undertaking appropriate actions that raise awareness; sometimes shows stewardship of his or her world

4. **Phase 4 (evaluating, creating):** Shows an active interest in global environmental issues; validates causes or concerns before offering support; takes a stand on matters of importance, undertaking appropriate actions that raise awareness of concerns through legitimate and appropriate means; shows stewardship, care, and responsibility for his or her world; thinks globally while acting locally

Discussion and Assessment Debrief

After conversation, students develop their own opinions about the assessment.

- *How did you evaluate this line from the assessment framework and why?*

- *How does the line from the assessment framework fit into the conversation?*

- *What does it mean for us? For the community? For the world?*

References and Resources

Frontline/World. (2009, June 23). *Ghana: Digital dumping ground* [Video file]. Accessed at www.pbs.org/frontlineworld/stories/ghana804/video/video _index.html on January 16, 2017.

page 2 of 3

McElvaney, K. (2014, February 27). Agbogbloshie: The world's largest e-waste dump—in pictures. *The Guardian*. Accessed at www.theguardian.com /environment/gallery/2014/feb/27/agbogbloshie-worlds-largest-e-waste -dump-in-pictures on January 16, 2017.

Minter, A. (2015, June 16). *Anatomy of a myth: The world's biggest e-waste dump isn't* [Blog post]. Accessed at http://shanghaiscrap.com/2015/06 /anatomy-of-a-myth-the-worlds-biggest-e-waste-dump-isnt on January 16, 2017.

Shibata, M. (2015, June 11). *Inside the world's biggest e-waste dump*. Accessed at http://motherboard.vice.com/read/inside-the-worlds-biggest-e-waste -dump on January 16, 2017.

Sim, M. (2015, June 25). *(UPDATE) Transforming Agbogbloshie: From toxic dump into model recycling center* [Blog post]. Accessed at www.pureearth.org /blog/photos-transforming-agbogbloshie-from-toxic-e-waste-dump-into -model-recycling-center on January 16, 2017.

Does Foreign Aid Always Help the Poor?

In an article at the World Economic Forum, Ana Swanson (2015) reports that the distribution of foreign aid is inefficient and unbalanced. Nobel Memorial Prize in Economic Sciences winner Sir Angus Deaton argues that trying to aid developing countries may actually slow their growth (Swanson, 2015). Foreign aid, unfortunately, has a history of not always being distributed to those most in need of it—if it's even distributed at all.

Deaton (Swanson, 2015) also argues that misuse of foreign aid can weaken government ties to people and leave them less accountable to those they serve. "Most governments depend on their people for taxes in order to run themselves and provide services to their people. Governments that get all their money from aid don't have that at all, and I think of that as very corrosive," Deaton claims (Swanson, 2015).

In the past, Zaire, Rwanda, Ethiopia, Somalia, and even the United States have been suspected of deploying foreign aid to support despotic regimes and personal interests of all sorts. This has prompted others to suggest bypassing corrupt governments and distributing food or funding directly among the people. Deaton posits that, "To get to the powerless, you often have to go through the powerful" (Swanson, 2015).

More Resources

Use the following resources to conduct your research.

- **"The Majority of International Aid Is Not Reaching the Countries That Need It the Most" (Morrison, 2014):** *www.independent.co.uk/news/world/africa /the-majority-of-international-aid-is-not-reaching-the-countries-that-need -it-the-most-9206182.html*

- **"Most Foreign Aid Does Not Go to Neediest Countries, Report Finds" (Vick, 2015):** *http://time.com/3897960/foreign-aid-poor-countries -extreme-poverty*

- **"The US Spends $35 Billion on Foreign Aid . . . but Where Does the Money Really Go?" (Amoros, 2015):** *http://mondoweiss.net/2015/11 /spends-billion-foreign*

- **"Top Ten Donors of Foreign Aid" (Maps of World, 2016):** *www.mapsofworld.com/world-top-ten/world-top-ten-doners-of -foreigner-aid-map.html*

Discussion Questions

Use the following questions to facilitate your classroom discussion.

- *What measures should we take to ensure our foreign aid is used to help those who need it most?*

page 1 of 3

- *Imagine you are in power in a country receiving foreign aid. How would you distribute and utilize the resources given to you?*

- *Do you believe that countries receiving aid should also be transparent with their sources about how it is spent? Why or why not?*

- *In what ways could foreign aid possibly encourage corruption and dependency from its government and people?*

- *How should we decide which countries are in most need of foreign aid? What parameters should we use to determine aid priority and why?*

Global Digital Citizen Assessment Framework

Use this four-phase assessment framework to establish the connection between altruistic service and problem finding.

1. **Phase 1 (awareness, connection, remembering):** Struggles to identify problems independently and frequently requires support and guidance

2. **Phase 2 (understanding, applying):** Describes and explains situations or issues on a local, regional, or global scale; can broadly consider the level of need and some of the potential impacts that his or her support could make

3. **Phase 3 (analyzing, evaluating):** Analyzes situations or issues on a local, regional, or global scale and breaks them down into their component parts; can identify and consider areas of need, the level of need, and some of the potential impacts that his or her support could make; investigates and researches the concern

4. **Phase 4 (evaluating, creating):** Analyzes and evaluates situations or issues on a local, regional, or global scale to identify areas of need; considers and evaluates the level of need and the impact that his or her support can make in resolving this; investigates and researches the concern to discern if the need is genuine, legitimate, and worthy of support

Discussion and Assessment Debrief

After conversation, students develop their own opinions about the assessment.

- *How did you evaluate this line from the assessment framework and why?*

- *How does the line from the assessment framework fit into the conversation?*

- *What does it mean for us? For the community? For the world?*

References

Amoros, R. (2015, November 4). *The US spends $35 billion on foreign aid . . . but where does the money really go?* Accessed at http://mondoweiss .net/2015/11/spends-billion-foreign on January 16, 2017.

Maps of World. (2016, June 1). *Top ten donors of foreign aid*. Accessed at www
.mapsofworld.com/world-top-ten/world-top-ten-doners-of-foreigner-aid
-map.html on January 16, 2017.

Morrison, S. (2014, March 21). The majority of international aid is not reaching the
countries that need it the most. *Independent*. Accessed at www
.independent.co.uk/news/world/africa/the-majority-of-international-aid
-is-not-reaching-the-countries-that-need-it-the-most-9206182.html on
January 16, 2017.

Swanson, A. (2015, October 23). *Does foreign aid always help the poor?* Accessed
at www.weforum.org/agenda/2015/10/does-foreign-aid-always-help-the
-poor on January 16, 2017.

Vick, K. (2015, May 27). Most foreign aid does not go to neediest countries, report
finds. *Time*. Accessed at http://time.com/3897960/foreign-aid-poor
-countries-extreme-poverty on January 16, 2017.

Empowering Global Citizens to Improve the World

Fernando Reimers (2016a) talks about the global citizen and his or her role in the future of world progress in a *Huffington Post* article. Reimers (2016a) reminds us that technology and its collaborative power lend global cultures all the power they need to come together over issues that affect us all. He also cautions us that some seek to misuse these advances. Says Reimers (2016a):

> Some of the risks we face together are the potential result of such misuse of humanity's scientific and technological advances. Risks [include] terrorism, cybercrime, organized crime, environmental degradation, government breakdown, corruption, illicit trade, fiscal crises, social inequality, racial and religious violence, among others.

The true global citizen, Reimers (2016a) says, is someone who can see the educational potential on both sides of the coin. He further cites that education has been key in empowering global citizens to be proactive in discovering the common thread of humanity that global cultures of all kinds share:

> The opportunity to do this now could not be more timely, more urgent indeed. The Sustainable Development Goals, adopted by world leaders at the last general assembly of the United Nations, provide an aspirational vision of how to construct a world without poverty, with more social inclusion, without violence, with prosperity and sustainability. This world is within reach, and an index is now available. (Reimers, 2016a)

In other words, in the end, the key lies in understanding.

More Resources

Use the following resources to conduct your research.

- **"Turning Students Into Global Citizens" (Reimers, 2016b):** *www.edweek .org/ew/articles/2016/08/03/turning-students-into-global-citizens.html*

- **"Flex Releases 2016 Global Citizenship Report" (PR Newswire, 2016):** *http://finance.yahoo.com/news/flex-releases-2016-global-citizenship -201500064.html*

- **"Why Startup Founders Ought to Be Global Citizens" (Upadhyaya, 2016):** *https://inc42.com/entrepreneurship/startup-founders-global-citizens*

- **"What Is Global Citizenship?" (IDEAS for Global Citizenship, n.d.):** *www.ideas-forum.org.uk/about-us/global-citizenship*

Discussion Questions

Use the following questions to facilitate your classroom discussion.

- *Why are global citizens regarded as the new citizens for our age?*

- *What do you personally feel are the most important characteristics of a global citizen?*

- *How important is it that global digital citizenship programs be taught in schools? Why?*

- *What kinds of beliefs or mindsets could possibly deter our society from becoming a global one in which we all support each other?*

- *What do you believe should be included in a program for educating global citizens?*

- *How do you practice global citizenship in your actions and relationships?*

- *What can you do to encourage global citizenship awareness in your own school?*

Global Digital Citizen Assessment Framework

Use this four-phase assessment framework to establish the connection between global citizenship and global awareness.

1. **Phase 1 (awareness, connection, remembering):** Has an awareness of some broader global issues; is sometimes considerate and may report inappropriate behavior

2. **Phase 2 (understanding, applying):** Displays characteristics of an emerging global citizen—shows some understanding of the cultural, religious, and gender differences; often shows respect for other peoples' customs and beliefs; demonstrates that he or she is developing an understanding of the value and worth of diversity; generally is intolerant of inappropriate behavior and occasionally takes steps to report it

3. **Phase 3 (analyzing, evaluating):** Displays characteristics of a developing global citizen—analyzes cultural, religious, and gender differences and uses them to guide his or her actions; shows respect for other peoples' customs and beliefs; will sometimes value and celebrate differences as part of the rich human tapestry; generally is intolerant of racist, abusive, sexist, or inappropriate behavior and sometimes takes steps to report it

4. **Phase 4 (evaluating, creating):** Displays the characteristics of a global citizen—considers and evaluates cultural, religious, and gender differences and mediates his or her actions and interactions by considering them; consistently shows respect and care for other peoples' customs and beliefs; values and celebrates differences as part of a rich human tapestry; shows intolerance of racist, abusive, sexist, or inappropriate behavior and, where possible, takes the appropriate steps to prevent or report it

Discussion and Assessment Debrief

After conversation, students develop their own opinions about the assessment.

- *How did you evaluate this line from the assessment framework and why?*

- *How does the line from the assessment framework fit into the conversation?*

- *What does it mean for us? For the community? For the world?*

References

IDEAS for Global Citizenship. (n.d.). *What is global citizenship?* Accessed at www.ideas-forum.org.uk/about-us/global-citizenship on January 16, 2017.

PR Newswire. (2016, August 2). *Flex releases 2016 Global Citizenship Report.* Accessed at http://finance.yahoo.com/news/flex-releases-2016-global -citizenship-201500064.html on January 16, 2017.

Reimers, F. M. (2016a, July 21). *Empowering global citizens to improve the world* [Blog post]. Accessed at www.huffingtonpost.com/fernando-reimers /empowering-global-citizen_b_11099352.html on January 9, 2017.

Reimers, F. M. (2016b, July 29). Turning students into global citizens. *Education Week.* Accessed at www.edweek.org/ew/articles/2016/08/03/turning -students-into-global-citizens.html on January 16, 2017.

Upadhyaya, V. (2016, August 9). *Why startup founders ought to be global citizens.* Accessed at https://inc42.com/entrepreneurship/startup-founders-global -citizens on January 16, 2017.

The Sandwich Man

This is the story of Allan Law, the Sandwich Man of Minneapolis. This former middle school teacher first discovered the homelessness problem in the inner-city schools where he taught, and it became a large concern for him. He wondered what he could do to help the homeless in his area, who often went days without food during the winter. So, he packed a row of freezers into his apartment, and he began making sandwiches. It was the beginning of great things.

Law drives around Minneapolis each evening, delivering sandwiches and other necessities to those living on the city's streets. He sleeps roughly two hours a night, and always in the back of his van. "I haven't slept in a bed in 13 years," Law states. "This is what I have to do, for the rest of my life" (Karmatube, n.d.).

Now heading a fully staffed and growing volunteer organization, Law receives donations from schools, churches, businesses, and the public. Through his organization, Law routinely delivers literally hundreds of thousands of sandwiches, blankets, socks, and mittens to the homeless in his city every year.

More Resources

Use the following resources to conduct your research.

- **"MRD Founder Mr. Allan Law" (Minneapolis Recreation Development, n.d.):** *www.363days.org/allanlaw.html*
- **"700,000 Sandwiches Later, This Man Is Still Helping the Homeless" (Huppert, 2015):** *www.usatoday.com/story/news/2015/04/20/inspiration -nation-sandwich-man/26096691*
- **The Sandwich Project:** *www.thesandwichprojectmn.org*

Discussion Questions

Use the following questions to facilitate your classroom discussion.

- *How does Law and the work he's doing set an example for others?*
- *Why do you think so many people have stepped forward to help Law in his cause?*
- *What are some other ways we can help those less fortunate than us?*
- *How would you go about beginning a delivery organization of your own in your city?*
- *Do you believe that what Law is doing is truly making a difference? Why or why not?*

page 1 of 2

Global Digital Citizen Assessment Framework

Use this four-phase assessment framework to establish the connection between personal responsibility and caring and compassion.

1. **Phase 1 (awareness, connection, remembering):** Sometimes shows care and consideration to the people with whom he or she interacts; sometimes offers support and shows gratitude and appreciation

2. **Phase 2 (understanding, applying):** Shows some care and consideration to others' needs; is sometimes supportive and will offer a critique that is appropriate and suitable; often shows gratitude and appreciation

3. **Phase 3 (analyzing, evaluating):** Shows caring and consideration for others' needs and the environment; is generally considerate in his or her actions and understands their impact; is generally suitably supportive and sometimes proactive; offers a critique that is generally appropriate and suitable; shows gratitude and appreciation

4. **Phase 4 (evaluating, creating):** Shows caring and is empathetic to others' needs and the environment; is considerate and deliberate in his or her actions, weighing their impact before enacting them; is always supportive, proactive, and considerate; offers a considerate critique that is appropriate and suitable; always shows genuine gratitude and appreciation

Discussion and Assessment Debrief

After conversation, students develop their own opinions about the assessment.

*   *How did you evaluate this line from the assessment framework and why?*

*   *How does the line from the assessment framework fit into the conversation?*

*   *What does it mean for us? For the community? For the world?*

References

Huppert, B. (2015, April 20). 700,000 sandwiches later, this man is still helping the homeless. *USA Today*. Accessed at www.usatoday.com/story/news/2015 /04/20/inspiration-nation-sandwich-man/26096691 on January 16, 2017.

Karmatube. (n.d.). *The sandwich man* [Video file]. Accessed at www.karmatube .org/videos.php?id=5975 on January 16, 2017.

Minneapolis Recreation Development. (n.d.). *MRD founder Mr. Allan Law*. Accessed at www.363days.org/allanlaw.html on January 16, 2017.

"What-Ifs" Surrounding Social Media's Role in Nicole Lovell's Death

Parents sometimes have a difficult choice to make when it comes to social media. These choices often come in the light of horribly tragic events like the death of Nicole Lovell, a student in West Virginia. As it turns out, she met one of her killers via the social media app Kik Messenger.

Parents are often exposed to this sad side of social media, and as such, base much of their opinions and actions on this kind of story. The *what-ifs* in this article build a foundation for what can be very meaningful and proactive discussions about social media between parents and their children.

More Resources

Use the following resources to conduct your research.

- **"Internet Safety Education: 10 Questions Parents Should Be Asking" (Graber, 2016a):** *www.huffingtonpost.com/diana-graber/internet-safety -education_b_9695250.html*

- **"10 Pros and Cons of Social Media" (TopTenSM Staff, n.d.):** *www.toptensocialmedia.com/social-media-social-buzz/10-pros-and-cons -of-social-media*

- **"Facebook, Instagram, and Social" (Common Sense Media, n.d.):** *www.commonsensemedia.org/social-media*

Discussion Questions

Use the following questions to facilitate your classroom discussion.

- *How do your parents feel about social media? How is it regulated in your home?*

- *Who do you know who has been threatened or bullied on social media? What could you do to help prevent this in the future?*

- *What would you do to educate or persuade your parents to see social media in a more positive light?*

- *How can you and your parents work together to keep safe on social media, and encourage others to do the same?*

Global Digital Citizen Assessment Framework

Use this four-phase assessment framework to establish the connection between digital citizenship and respect and responsibility for oneself.

page 1 of 2

1. **Phase 1 (awareness, connection, remembering):** Has an awareness of some of the online risks and appropriate strategies for personal online safety; sometimes takes steps to protect him- or herself

2. **Phase 2 (understanding, applying):** Frequently applies appropriate strategies in his or her online behavior and to minimize exposure to risk; takes some steps to protect his or her integrity, privacy, data, or identity; sometimes seeks support or reports abuse

3. **Phase 3 (analyzing, evaluating):** Is often considerate of his or her online behavior; takes steps to protect his or her integrity, privacy, data, and identity; analyzes and evaluates his or her situation and takes steps to minimize his or her exposure to risk; often seeks support and reports abuse to relevant authorities

4. **Phase 4 (evaluating, creating):** Shows regular deliberation and consideration of his or her online behavior; takes all suitable steps to protect his or her integrity, privacy, data, and identity; evaluates his or her situation and is both proactive and reactive toward minimizing his or her exposure to risk; seeks support and reports abuse to relevant authorities

Discussion and Assessment Debrief

After conversation, students develop their own opinions about the assessment.

- *How did you evaluate this line from the assessment framework and why?*

- *How does the line from the assessment framework fit into the conversation?*

- *What does it mean for us? For the community? For the world?*

References and Resources

Common Sense Media. (n.d.). *Facebook, Instagram, and social.* Accessed at www.commonsensemedia.org/social-media on January 16, 2017.

Graber, D. (2016a, April 15). *Internet safety education: 10 questions parents should be asking* [Blog post]. Accessed at www.huffingtonpost.com/diana -graber/internet-safety-education_b_9695250.html on January 16, 2017.

Graber, D. (2016b, February 5). *"What if's" surrounding social media's role in Nicole Lovell's death* [Blog post]. Accessed at www.huffingtonpost.com/diana -graber/what-ifs-surrounding-soci_b_9162348.html on January 16, 2017.

TopTenSM Staff. (n.d.). *10 pros and cons of social media.* Accessed at www.toptensocialmedia.com/social-media-social-buzz/10-pros-and -cons-of-social-media on January 16, 2017.

Global Matters are adapted from content originally published by the
Global Digital Citizen Foundation (https://globaldigitalcitizen.org) © 2017. Used with permission.

Latest Ocean Warming Review Reveals Extent of Impacts on Nature and Humans

A 2016 report by the International Union for Conservation of Nature (IUCN) confirms a grim reality for our planet: the continuing warming of our oceans is having a devastating impact on our planet's entire ecosystem, and the problem will only get worse. The overview of the article says:

> Ocean warming is affecting humans in direct ways and the impacts are already being felt, including effects on fish stocks and crop yields, more extreme weather events and increased risk from water-borne diseases, according to what has been called the most comprehensive review available on the issue. (IUCN, 2016)

Inger Andersen, director general of the IUCN, adds, "The only way to preserve the rich diversity of marine life, and to safeguard the protection and resources the ocean provides us with, is to cut greenhouse gas emissions rapidly and substantially" (IUCN, 2016).

More Resources

Use the following resources to conduct your research.

- *"Global Warming" (ScienceDaily, n.d.):* www.sciencedaily.com/terms/global_warming.htm

- *"Main Greenhouse Gases" (Center for Climate and Energy Solutions, n.d.):* www.c2es.org/facts-figures/main-ghgs

- *"Global Greenhouse Gas Emissions Data" (United States Environmental Protection Agency, n.d.):* www.epa.gov/ghgemissions/global-greenhouse-gas-emissions-data

- *"2016 May Be Hottest Year Yet: Global Warming at an 'Unprecedented' Pace in a Millenium* [sic]*, NASA Says" (E, 2016):* www.natureworldnews.com/articles/27988/20160902/2016-hottest-year-global-warming-unprecedented-pace-millenium-nasa.htm

Discussion Questions

Use the following questions to facilitate your classroom discussion.

- *What outcome would you predict if our oceans continue to warm if nothing can be done to stop it?*

- *What have we done in the past in global and international communities to guard against global warming? How successful have these efforts been?*

page 1 of 3

- *How do your own personal activities or those of your family affect global warming?*

- *What are some of the hidden or unseen costs and effects of global warming?*

Global Digital Citizen Assessment Framework

Use this four-phase assessment framework to establish the connection between environmental stewardship and global awareness and action.

1. **Phase 1 (awareness, connection, remembering):** Has an awareness of some of the environmental issues and, when encouraged, may participate in activities to reduce or raise awareness of them

2. **Phase 2 (understanding, applying):** Has an interest in and understanding of some environmental issues; supports local environmental activities, sometimes taking a stand on significant issues

3. **Phase 3 (analyzing, evaluating):** Shows an interest in global environmental issues and investigates causes or concerns before offering support; often takes a stand on current matters, undertaking appropriate actions that raise awareness; sometimes shows stewardship of his or her world

4. **Phase 4 (evaluating, creating):** Shows an active interest in global environmental issues; validates causes or concerns before offering support; takes a stand on matters of importance, undertaking appropriate actions that raise awareness of concerns through legitimate and appropriate means; shows stewardship, care, and responsibility for his or her world; thinks globally while acting locally

Discussion and Assessment Debrief

After conversation, students develop their own opinions about the assessment.

- *How did you evaluate this line from the assessment framework and why?*

- *How does the line from the assessment framework fit into the conversation?*

- *What does it mean for us? For the community? For the world?*

References

Center for Climate and Energy Solutions. (n.d.). *Main greenhouse gases*. Accessed at www.c2es.org/facts-figures/main-ghgs on January 16, 2017.

E, J. (2016, September 2). *2016 may be hottest year yet: Global warming at an 'unprecedented' pace in a millenium* [sic]*, NASA says*. Accessed at www.natureworldnews.com/articles/27988/20160902/2016-hottest-year-global-warming-unprecedented-pace-millenium-nasa.htm on January 16, 2017.

International Union for Conservation of Nature. (2016, September 6). *Latest ocean warming review reveals extent of impacts on nature and humans.* Accessed at www.sciencedaily.com/releases/2016/09/160906085016.htm on January 16, 2017.

ScienceDaily. (n.d.). *Global warming.* Accessed at www.sciencedaily.com/terms /global_warming.htm on January 9, 2017.

United States Environmental Protection Agency. (n.d.). *Global greenhouse gas emissions data.* Accessed at www.epa.gov/ghgemissions/global -greenhouse-gas-emissions-data on January 16, 2017.

Has Responsibility Left the Building?

Catholic High School for Boys in Little Rock, Arkansas, has taken extreme measures to ensure its young students are learning to handle their own affairs. The school has essentially banned parents from bringing any items forgotten at home by their sons in an attempt to foster a sense of personal responsibility among the students.

A sign outside the school reads: "If you are dropping off your son's forgotten lunch, books, homework, equipment, etc., please TURN AROUND and exit the building. Your son will learn to problem solve in your absence."

This measure has sparked both kudos and outrage across the parental community. Some parents are lauding the school's efforts to teach students self-reliance, while others are shocked by what they refer to as a *disgusting* school policy.

More Resources

Use the following resources to conduct your research.

- **"Promoting Responsible and Ethical Digital Citizens" (McGilvery, 2012):** *www.educationworld.com/a_tech/responsible-student-technology-use.shtml*

- **"Teaching Global Digital Citizenship? Use These 10 Essential Questions" (Crockett, 2017):** *https://globaldigitalcitizen.org/teaching-global-digital -citizenship-10-essential-questions*

- **"Are We Teaching Responsibility Or Just Obedience?" (Kline, n.d.):** *www.changekidslives.org/thoughts-2*

Discussion Questions

Use the following questions to facilitate your classroom discussion.

- *What is your opinion of the measures this school has taken to ensure student responsibility?*

- *Why would a school decide to take this approach? What may have caused the school to make this decision?*

- *What would happen if your school imposed the same rules? What would your parents' reaction be?*

- *How can the school ensure that students take personal responsibilities seriously without having to impose strict guidelines and rules for compliance?*

- *Do you feel that what the school is doing is an ethical and effective approach, or a violation of rights?*

page 1 of 2

Global Digital Citizen Assessment Framework

Use this four-phase assessment framework to establish the connection between personal responsibility and accountability.

1. **Phase 1 (awareness, connection, remembering):** Shows awareness that his or her actions affect others and that others' actions affect him or her; occasionally accepts responsibility for his or her actions and attempts to change his or her behaviors

2. **Phase 2 (understanding, applying):** Shows awareness that he or she has an impact on a personal and local scale; considers his or her behaviors and actions, often taking responsibility, and applies changes to behaviors and observes results

3. **Phase 3 (analyzing, evaluating):** Analyzes the impact of his or her behaviors and actions on a personal, local, and global scale; frequently takes responsibility and often undertakes measures to avoid, reduce, or minimize impacts

4. **Phase 4 (evaluating, creating):** Evaluates the impact of his or her behaviors and actions on a personal, local, and global scale; accepts responsibility and is proactive in undertaking what measures he or she can to avoid, reduce, or minimize impacts

Discussion and Assessment Debrief

After conversation, students develop their own opinions about the assessment.

- *How did you evaluate this line from the assessment framework and why?*

- *How does the line from the assessment framework fit into the conversation?*

- *What does it mean for us? For the community? For the world?*

References and Resources

Crockett, L. W. (2017, February 8). *Teaching global digital citizenship? Use these 10 essential questions*. Accessed at https://globaldigitalcitizen.org/teaching -global-digital-citizenship-10-essential-questions on June 1, 2017.

Kline, T. (n.d.). *Are we teaching responsibility or just obedience?* Accessed at www.changekidslives.org/thoughts-2 on June 1, 2017.

McGilvery, C. (2012). Promoting responsible and ethical digital citizens. *Education World*. Accessed at www.educationworld.com/a_tech /responsible-student-technology-use.shtml on January 16, 2017.

Starnes, T. (2016, August 18). SHOCKING! School makes kids take personal responsibility! *Fox News*. Accessed at www.foxnews.com/opinion /2016/08/18/shocking-school-makes-kids-take-personal-responsibility .html on January 16, 2017.

Global Matters are adapted from content originally published by the
Global Digital Citizen Foundation (https://globaldigitalcitizen.org) © 2017. Used with permission.

Appendix B

Activity Sheets

Each of the activities in this appendix represents a conversation relating to one of the guidelines of the primary, middle, or secondary school agreements. These activities are meant to stir ideas and debates that foster discussion about the ideals of the agreements. Visit **go.SolutionTree.com/technology** to download free copies.

Primary School Activity Sheets

Use these primary school activity sheets to foster discussion.

Looking After Myself

Each list item corresponds with an entry in your digital citizenship guidelines. Review the guideline and accompanying scenario, and answer the question.

1. *I will only go on the computer when I have permission.*

    You have a free activity period and want to use the computer to play a game. **What should you do before logging on?**

2. *I will only go to pages I am allowed to go to.*

    You are using one of the school computers to do an activity, and you know that your teacher has a list of webpages that students are allowed to use in class. **What should you do before starting to visit webpages?**

3. *I will only share pictures and stories about myself when my teacher tells me to.*

    You want to share pictures from your summer vacation with your friends, but you're not sure how to do it. A friend says he knows how, but your teacher has asked you to check with her first, before you post anything. **Who should you ask to help you?**

4. *I will talk to my parents and teacher about all of my online friends.*

    You just made a new friend online, and he is asking you to share some pictures. **Whom should you talk to about your new friend and why?**

5. *I will tell my teacher or parents if anyone is unkind to me on the computer.*

    Someone responded to one of your posted pictures with a mean comment. This person is calling your friends rude names as well. **Who do you talk to about the bully?**

Looking After Others

Each list item corresponds with an entry in your digital citizenship guidelines. Review the guideline and accompanying scenario, and answer the question.

1. *I will only say nice things about people.*

    Someone you know has been called names by another student. **What do you do?**

2. *I will ask before I share a picture or story about a person.*

    One of your friends created a picture and poem that you really like and sent it to you. You want to share it with others. **What should you do first?**

3. *I will only go to places that are nice, and I will tell my parents or teacher if I go to a place that is nasty, unkind, or rude.*

    You are using one of the school computers, and suddenly you find yourself on a website that contains frightening pictures and pop-ups. You don't know how you ended up there. **Who should you tell about it?**

Looking After Property

Each list item corresponds with an entry in your digital citizenship guidelines. Review the guideline and accompanying scenario, and answer the question.

1. *I will not download movies, games, or music.*

    You just saw a movie that you really like, and someone you know has told you where you can download it, plus other things like music and games, for free. **Do you visit this site and download what you want?**

2. *I will check that the information I get online is correct.*

    You are searching for something online. You come across a website that claims to be the expert source of lots of things. It even ranks number one in a Google search. **Do you trust the site, or ask your teacher or parents to help you?**

3. *I will not leave rude or unkind messages on other people's spaces.*

    You and your classmates, with your teacher's guidance, set up your first profile pages on a social media site. As an exercise, your teacher asks you to visit some pages and check out what other students are up to. **What kind of comments and messages will you leave them and why?**

Digital citizenship guidelines are adapted from content originally published by the Global Digital Citizen Foundation (https://globaldigitalcitizen.org) © 2017. Used with permission.

Growing Global Digital Citizens © 2018 Solution Tree Press • SolutionTree.com
Visit **go.SolutionTree.com/technology** to download this free reproducible.

Middle School Activity Sheets

Use these middle school activity sheets to foster discussion.

Looking After Myself

Each list item corresponds with an entry in your digital citizenship guidelines. Review the guideline and accompanying scenario, and answer the question.

1. *I will choose online names that are suitable and respectful.*

   Your friends are all using a new social media site and want you to join. The site only shows the user's profile name. You must create a name that is based on your actual name, but is incomplete enough to protect your identity. **What name would you use and why?**

2. *I will only invite people I actually know in the physical world to be my friends in the online world.*

   You are on a new social media site, and you receive a friendship request from a person you don't know. The profile says this person is the same age as you and has a very good-looking profile picture. **Should you accept the person's request? Why did you make your decision?**

3. *I will only visit sites that are appropriate, and I will respect the rules that websites have about age. Some sites are only for adults. If I don't feel comfortable showing the website to my parents or grandparents, then it is inappropriate.*

   One of your friends has joined an adult dating site. The site has an age restriction of eighteen years old, and your friend lied about his birthdate to join the site. Your friend received a date invitation from a member of the dating site. **What advice would you give to your friend?**

4. *I will set my privacy settings so only the people I know can see me or my personal information.*

   One of your classmates is making jokes about your last holiday. You haven't ever spoken to her about it, and you think she might have been looking at your social media profile and pictures. You are not friends with her, but your privacy settings are set at Friends of Friends. **What does the privacy setting Friends of Friends mean, and is this the best setting for you to use?**

5. *I will only put information online that is appropriate and post only pictures that are suitable. Not everyone seeing my profile or pictures will be friendly.*

   One of your friends posted a very revealing picture of himself, wearing only his underwear. He had lots of likes and comments. He is encouraging you to put up similar pictures. **What should you do? What advice should you give to your friend?**

Growing Global Digital Citizens © 2018 Solution Tree Press • SolutionTree.com
Visit **go.SolutionTree.com/technology** to download this free reproducible.

6. *I will always report anything that happens online that makes me feel uncomfortable or unhappy.*

   A slightly older person has been chatting with you online. She said she is interested in the same activities, sports, and hobbies as you. She has given you good advice in the past, but recently she is asking you if you are alone and in your bedroom. She also asked if you could meet up somewhere. **What should you do?**

7. *I will talk to trusted adults, like my parents and teachers, about my online experiences. This includes both the good and the bad experiences.*

   One of the people in your friendship group posted pictures of you and made some funny comments. He didn't ask if he could post your pictures, and some of your other friends are adding replies and likes. The comments use humor, but are quite personal and hurtful. You want this to stop, but you are scared that you might lose friends. **Whom should you talk to and why?**

Looking After Others

Each list item corresponds with an entry in your digital citizenship guidelines. Review the guideline and accompanying scenario, and answer the question.

1. *I will show I care by not flaming (sending hurtful or inflammatory messages) other people, or forwarding messages that are unkind or inappropriate.*

   You have been included in an email list which sends around funny jokes, memes, and images. At first, the jokes were quite funny, but recently they have been racist and degrading. Some of the images have been pornographic. You used to send them on to your friends and still have all of them in your school email account. **What should you do?**

2. *I will not get involved in conversations that are unkind, mean, or bullying.*

   A group of your classmates is standing in a circle looking at pictures on a phone. One of them says, "Send them to me! Send them!" and laughs. The rest of the group agrees and asks for them to be sent to everyone. The pictures are partly undressed selfies of one of the people in your grade. **What should you do?**

3. *I will report any conversations I see that are unkind, mean, or bullying. I can imagine if the things being written were about me. If I find them offensive, then they are inappropriate.*

   One of the students in your class has been annoying. She thinks she is funny and popular. One of your friends posted some very nasty things about her on his social media profile. Your friend wants you to like or reply to his post. **What should you do? Ignore it, post a comment, or report it?**

page 2 of 4

4. *I will show my respect for others by avoiding websites that are disrespectful because they show people behaving inappropriately or illegally—or are racist, bigoted, or unkind. If I visit one by accident, I will close it and tell my teacher or an adult.*

You are seated in the middle of the room in one of your classes at school. The class is boring, and you are surfing the Internet. You go to a website, and there are pop-ups that contain pornographic images and link to pornographic websites and live chatrooms. **What should you do?**

5. *I will show respect for others' privacy by not trying to get into their online spaces without invitation, and by not stalking them or copying their pictures.*

You really like one of the students in your grade level. She posts lots of pictures and videos on her social media profile. She has not set the privacy settings to allow only friends to see the pictures. You could send a friendship request, but she might reject it or block you, or you could continue to anonymously visit her profile. **What should you do?**

Looking After Property

Each list item corresponds with an entry in your digital citizenship guidelines. Review the guideline and accompanying scenario, and answer the question.

1. *I will not steal other people's property. It's easy to download music, games, and movies, but piracy (downloading media that I have not bought) is just the name given to stealing online.*

The latest album by your favorite artist comes out on iTunes. The album is a new release and is at the premium price, which you cannot afford. Only the complete album is available for purchase and not the individual songs. You know you can find copies of the music online. **Do you search for and download the music?**

2. *I will not share with other people the music, movies, games, and other software that I own.*

You have a friend come over to your place. You muck around playing music on your MP3 player. Your friend asks you for a copy of your music collection. **Do you give it to him?**

3. *I will check that the information I use is correct. Anyone can say anything on the web, so I need to use reliable websites to check that my research is correct. When in doubt, I will ask my teacher or parents.*

It's Thursday evening, and your assignment is due at 8:30 Friday morning. You have only framed out the work. You're panicking and talk to one of your friends. She said you can download a similar assignment from a specific website, change a few words, and then send that in as your own. **Why shouldn't you do this?**

page 3 of 4

4. *I will look after other people's websites, acting appropriately when visiting them, not making changes or vandalizing them, and reporting any damage that I find.*

You have been given someone else's serial number, which is used as the registration key for the latest game. The game producer is a huge multinational that makes vast profits each year. The game is free to download but requires the registration key, which you are meant to purchase to play beyond the basic game. **Do you use the key? Why or why not?**

page 4 of 4

Digital citizenship guidelines are adapted from content originally published by the
Global Digital Citizen Foundation (https://globaldigitalcitizen.org) © 2017. Used with permission.

High School Activity Sheets

Use these high school activity sheets to foster discussion.

Respect for Myself

Review the following digital citizenship guidelines and answer the accompanying questions.

I will show respect for myself through my actions. I will select online names that are appropriate. I will consider the information and images I post online. I will not post personal information about my life, experiences, experimentation, or relationships. I will not be obscene.

1. How do your online actions in social media environments affect you in the physical world?

2. What are the repercussions of behaving inappropriately online?

3. Why is it important to consider privacy and security when posting personal information and content online?

Responsibility for Myself

Review the following digital citizenship guidelines and answer the accompanying questions.

I will ensure that the information I post online will not put me at risk. I will not publish my personal details, contact details, or a schedule of my activities. I will report any attacks or inappropriate behavior directed at me. I will protect passwords, accounts, and resources.

1. What are some of the ways you can protect yourself from phishing, flaming, or cyberbullying attacks?

2. How can you generate passwords that are easy to remember yet difficult for others to hack? What guidelines should you use?

Respect for Others

Review the following digital citizenship guidelines and answer the accompanying questions.

I will show respect to others. I will not use electronic mediums to flame, bully, harass, or stalk other people. I will show respect for other people in my choice of websites. I will not visit sites that are degrading, pornographic, racist, or inappropriate. I will not abuse my rights of access, and I will not enter other people's private spaces or areas.

page 1 of 3

1. What are the immediate and hidden consequences of subjecting someone to online mistreatment?

2. Why do bullies prefer to harass people online rather than in person?

3. How does frequenting inappropriate websites harm those the site victimizes or abuses?

4. What are rights of access, and how are they granted and monitored?

5. What are the short- and long-term consequences of abusing your rights of access on a site?

6. What is entering another's private online space equivalent to in the physical world, and why is it unethical and dangerous?

Responsibility for Others

Review the following digital citizenship guidelines and answer the accompanying questions.

I will protect others by reporting abuse, not forwarding inappropriate materials or communications, and not visiting sites that are degrading, pornographic, racist, or inappropriate.

1. Why should you report abuse when you see it happen online?

2. How does not acting out against online abuse perpetuate the behavior?

3. What are the emotional and psychological effects of online abuse?

4. Why is it important not to forward inappropriate information and communications about yourself or others?

Respect for Property

Review the following digital citizenship guidelines and answer the accompanying questions.

I will request permission to use resources. I will suitably cite any and all use of websites, books, media, and so on. I will acknowledge all primary and secondary sources. I will validate information. I will use and abide by the fair-use rules.

1. Why should you obtain verbal or written permission before you use others' material?

2. What procedures can you use to suitably cite media sources you use?

3. How can you make sure the information you find online is correct?

4. What are fair-use rules, and whom do they protect?

page 2 of 3

Responsibility for Property

Review the following digital citizenship guidelines and answer the accompanying questions.

I will request to use the software and media others produce. I will use free and open-source alternatives rather than pirating software. I will purchase, license, and register all software. I will purchase my music and other media, and refrain from distributing these in a manner that violates their licenses. I will act with integrity.

1. What are some of the damaging effects and costs of illegally pirating media?

2. Why should you never share your media with others who ask for it?

3. How can you search for free and open-source materials that you can use without copyright?

4. What can you do to check if the media you find online is protected by copyright?

5. What are the consequences of ignoring this?

Digital citizenship guidelines are adapted from content originally published by the Global Digital Citizen Foundation (https://globaldigitalcitizen.org) © 2017. Used with permission.

Growing Global Digital Citizens © 2018 Solution Tree Press • SolutionTree.com
Visit **go.SolutionTree.com/technology** to download this free reproducible.

Digital Citizenship Agreements

This appendix includes the full text of the digital citizenship agreements included in chapter 3 for primary, middle, and high schools. It also includes the professional and personal digital citizenship agreements we depicted in chapters 4 and 6. Visit **go.SolutionTree.com/technology** to download free copies.

Digital Citizenship Primary School Agreement

This digital citizenship agreement is best suited for primary or elementary school—level students. You can use it in its current form or adapt it to create a version that better fits your school's unique culture and needs.

Looking After Myself

- *I will only go on the computer when I have permission.*
- *I will only go to pages I am allowed to go to.*
- *I will only share pictures and stories about myself when my teacher tells me to.*
- *I will talk to my parents and teacher about all of my online friends.*
- *I will tell my teacher or parents if anyone is unkind to me on the computer.*

Looking After Others

- *I will only say nice things about people.*
- *I will ask before I share a picture or story about a person.*
- *I will only go to places that are nice, and I will tell my parents or teacher if I go to a place that is nasty, unkind, or rude.*

Looking After Property

- *I will not download movies, games, or music.*
- *I will check that the information I get online is correct.*
- *I will not leave rude or unkind messages on other people's spaces.*

Digital citizenship guidelines are adapted from content originally published by the Global Digital Citizen Foundation (https://globaldigitalcitizen.org) © 2017. Used with permission.

Growing Global Digital Citizens © 2018 Solution Tree Press • SolutionTree.com
Visit **go.SolutionTree.com/technology** to download this free reproducible.

Digital Citizenship Middle School Agreement

This digital citizenship agreement is best suited for middle school–level students. You can use it in its current form or adapt it to create a version that better fits your school's unique culture and needs.

Looking After Myself

- *I will choose online names that are suitable and respectful.*

- *I will only invite people I actually know in the physical world to be my friends in the online world.*

- *I will only visit sites that are appropriate, and I will respect the rules that websites have about age. Some sites are only for adults. If I don't feel comfortable showing the website to my parents or grandparents, then it is inappropriate.*

- *I will set my privacy settings so only the people I know can see me or my personal information.*

- *I will only put information online that is appropriate and post only pictures that are suitable. Not everyone seeing my profile or pictures will be friendly.*

- *I will always report anything that happens online that makes me feel uncomfortable or unhappy.*

- *I will talk to trusted adults, like my parents and teachers, about my online experiences. This includes both the good and the bad experiences.*

Looking After Others

- *I will show I care by not flaming (sending hurtful or inflammatory messages) other people, or forwarding messages that are unkind or inappropriate.*

- *I will not get involved in conversations that are unkind, mean, or bullying.*

- *I will report any conversations I see that are unkind, mean, or bullying. I can imagine if the things being written were about me. If I find them offensive, then they are inappropriate.*

- *I will show my respect for others by avoiding websites that are disrespectful because they show people behaving inappropriately or illegally—or are racist, bigoted, or unkind. If I visit one by accident, I will close it and tell my teacher or an adult.*

- *I will show respect for others' privacy by not trying to get into their online spaces without invitation, and by not stalking them or copying their pictures.*

page 1 of 2

Looking After Property

- *I will not steal other people's property. It's easy to download music, games, and movies, but piracy (downloading media that I have not bought) is just the name given to stealing online.*

- *I will not share with other people the music, movies, games, and other software that I own.*

- *I will check that the information I use is correct. Anyone can say anything on the web, so I need to use reliable websites to check that my research is correct. When in doubt, I will ask my teacher or parents.*

- *I will look after other people's websites, acting appropriately when visiting them, not making changes or vandalizing them, and reporting any damage that I find.*

By signing this agreement, I undertake to always act in a manner that is respectful to myself and others, and to act appropriately and in a moral and ethical manner.

I, _____, agree to follow the principles of digital citizenship outlined in this agreement and accept that failing to follow these tenets will have consequences.

Signed: _____ Date: _____ / _____ / _____

Digital citizenship guidelines are adapted from content originally published by the Global Digital Citizen Foundation (https://globaldigitalcitizen.org) © 2017. Used with permission.

Growing Global Digital Citizens © 2018 Solution Tree Press • SolutionTree.com
Visit **go.SolutionTree.com/technology** to download this free reproducible.

Digital Citizenship High School Agreement

This digital citizenship agreement is best suited for high school–level students. You can use it in its current form or adapt it to create a version that better fits your school's unique culture and needs.

Respect for Myself

I will show respect for myself through my actions. I will select online names that are appropriate. I will consider the information and images I post online. I will not post personal information about my life, experiences, experimentation, or relationships. I will not be obscene.

Responsibility for Myself

I will ensure that the information I post online will not put me at risk. I will not publish my personal details, contact details, or a schedule of my activities. I will report any attacks or inappropriate behavior directed at me. I will protect passwords, accounts, and resources.

Respect for Others

I will show respect to others. I will not use electronic mediums to flame, bully, harass, or stalk other people. I will show respect for other people in my choice of websites. I will not visit sites that are degrading, pornographic, racist, or inappropriate. I will not abuse my rights of access, and I will not enter other people's private spaces or areas.

Responsibility for Others

I will protect others by reporting abuse, not forwarding inappropriate materials or communications, and not visiting sites that are degrading, pornographic, racist, or inappropriate.

Respect for Property

I will request permission to use resources. I will suitably cite any and all use of websites, books, media, and so on. I will acknowledge all primary and secondary sources. I will validate information. I will use and abide by fair-use rules.

Responsibility for Property

I will request to use the software and media others produce. I will use free and open-source alternatives rather than pirating software. I will purchase, license, and register

page 1 of 2

Growing Global Digital Citizens © 2018 Solution Tree Press • SolutionTree.com
Visit **go.SolutionTree.com/technology** to download this free reproducible.

all software. I will purchase my music and other media, and refrain from distributing these in a manner that violates their licenses. I will act with integrity.

By signing this agreement, I undertake to always act in a manner that is respectful to myself and others, and to act appropriately and in a moral and ethical manner.

I, _____, agree to follow the principles of digital citizenship outlined in this agreement and accept that failing to follow these tenets will have consequences.

Signed: _____ Date: _____ / _____ / _____

Digital citizenship guidelines are adapted from content originally published by the Global Digital Citizen Foundation (https://globaldigitalcitizen.org) © 2017. Used with permission.

Growing Global Digital Citizens © 2018 Solution Tree Press • SolutionTree.com
Visit **go.SolutionTree.com/technology** to download this free reproducible.

Digital Citizenship Personal Guidelines

This digital citizenship agreement is best suited for parents, guardians, and other members of the wider community. You can use it in its current form or adapt it to create a version that better fits your locality's unique culture and needs.

Respect for Myself By

- *Showing respect for myself through my actions*
- *Considering what personal information about my life, experiences, experimentation, or relationships I post*
- *Considering the materials that I post online and how these may reflect on myself, my family, and the wider community, including my work*
- *Considering the sites that I visit and how they may reflect on me as a person and as a member of the family*
- *Not being obscene, degrading, rude, or inappropriate*

Responsibility for Myself By

- *Considering the impact of my actions and behaviors and consequences of my actions on myself and my family*
- *Being balanced in my use of technology and being informed and aware of both the risks and benefits of my technology use*
- *Separating my personal and professional use of technology*
- *Protecting my identity; ensuring that the information, images, and materials I post online will not put me or my family at risk*
- *Considering the personal information I have published and the social networks that I have joined; being aware that the audience may be broader and wider than I intended*
- *Taking suitable steps to ensure my online and offline safety and privacy*
- *Taking steps to protect my data*
- *Reporting any attacks or inappropriate behavior directed at me and seeking support from appropriate people or organizations*
- *Protecting passwords, bank and credit card accounts, and resources*

Respect for Others By

- *Using appropriate language and judgment when sending emails, posts, or messages—even when angry*

page 1 of 3

- *Selecting appropriate mediums and social networks for my personal communications, showing consideration to others, and understanding the limitations of the mediums*
- *Not using electronic mediums to flame, bully, harass, or stalk other people*
- *Being conscientious in my choice of websites; avoiding, whenever possible, visiting sites that are inappropriate, degrading, pornographic, or racist*
- *Not abusing my rights of access*
- *Being a role model for appropriate use of technology*

Responsibility for Others By

- *Guiding, educating, and supporting my family and friends in the appropriate use of technology*
- *Modeling balanced use of technologies; setting an example of restraint, appropriate use, balance, and respect*
- *Being intolerant of abuse whether directed at or stemming from my family and friends; taking appropriate steps to deal with such, including reporting abuse*
- *Balancing the often-conflicting needs for safety and privacy in our use of technology*
- *Taking appropriate steps to ensure the safety and privacy of my family and friends; seeking permission beforehand to post their personal information, photos, videos, and so on*
- *Limiting access to information to those who should have access to it; considering the privacy settings and groups that material is published to*
- *Moderating unacceptable materials and conversations; reporting conversations that are inappropriate or unacceptable*
- *Not forwarding inappropriate materials or communications*

Respect for Property By

- *Modeling appropriate purchasing of software and media; being intolerant of piracy of materials including music, movies, and other media by my family and friends*
- *Requesting permission to use resources; respecting and abiding by copyright, intellectual property, and patent*
- *Validating information and checking the accuracy of advisory posts and emails I receive*
- *Guiding and supporting my family and friends*

Responsibility for Property By

- *Being aware of my legal rights in regard to using copyrighted media; understanding my rights for backup and distribution of different media within my immediate family*

- *Suitably protecting other people's rights to protect their copyright and intellectual property*

- *Using only appropriately obtained, licensed, and registered software and media*

- *Suitably protecting our systems to ensure their security and integrity*

- *Reporting vandalism and damage*

By signing this agreement, I undertake to always act in a manner that is respectful to myself and others, and to act appropriately and in a moral and ethical manner.

I, _____, agree to follow the principles of digital citizenship outlined in this agreement and accept that failing to follow these tenets will have consequences.

Signed: _____ Date: _____ / _____ / _____

Digital Citizenship Professional Guidelines

This digital citizenship agreement is best suited for teachers, administrators, and other staff of the school community. You can use it in its current form or adapt it to create a version that better fits your school's unique culture and needs.

Respect for Myself By

- *Showing respect for myself through my actions*
- *Considering the information and images that I post online and how these may reflect on myself, my family, and my company*
- *Considering what personal information about my life, experiences, experimentation, or relationships I post*
- *Not being obscene, degrading, rude, or inappropriate*

Responsibility for Myself By

- *Considering the impact of my actions and behaviors and consequences of my actions on myself, my family, and my company*
- *Separating my personal and professional use of technology*
- *Protecting my identity; ensuring that the information, images, and materials I post online will not put me at risk*
- *Considering the personal and professional information I have published and that the audience may be broader and wider than I intended*
- *Taking suitable steps to ensure my online safety and protecting the integrity and security of my data*
- *Reporting any attacks or inappropriate behavior directed at me and seeking support from appropriate people or organizations*
- *Protecting passwords, bank and credit card accounts, and resources*
- *Being aware of the consequences of my actions*

Respect for Others By

- *Using professional language and judgment when sending emails, posts, or messages—even when angry*
- *Selecting appropriate mediums for my communications, showing consideration to others, and understanding the limitations of different mediums*
- *Not using electronic mediums to flame, bully, harass, or stalk other people*

page 1 of 3

- *Being conscientious in my choice of websites and avoiding, whenever possible, sites that are inappropriate (for example, sites that are degrading, pornographic, or racist)*

- *Not abusing my rights of access; avoiding entering private spaces or using surveillance systems in a manner that abuses privacy*

Responsibility for Others By

- *Protecting others by reporting abuse and not forwarding inappropriate materials or communications*

- *Moderating unacceptable materials and conversations and reporting conversations that are inappropriate or unacceptable*

- *Taking appropriate steps to ensure the safety and privacy of my colleagues and clients; seeking permission before posting their personal and corporate information*

- *Ensuring that the information held in trust is suitably protected and only used for its intended purpose, and then disposing of said information appropriately*

- *Limiting access to information to those who legitimately need it, and protecting it from others; refraining from passing said information to third parties*

Respect for Property By

- *Requesting permission to use resources; respecting and abiding by copyright, intellectual property, and patent*

- *Citing any and all use of websites, books, and other media and acknowledging all primary and secondary sources*

- *Validating information*

- *Being transparent in my licensing of software, media, and materials*

Responsibility for Property By

- *Maintaining professional awareness of my rights to use other people's material*

- *Suitably protecting my and my company's copyright, intellectual property, and patent*

- *Using appropriately obtained, licensed, and registered software and media*

- *Using media within the limitations of their licenses and refraining from distributing these in a manner that violates these conditions*

- *Suitably protecting my systems to ensure their security and integrity*

- *Reporting vandalism and damage*

By signing this agreement, I undertake to always act in a manner that is respectful to myself and others, and to act appropriately and in a moral and ethical manner.

I, _____, agree to follow the principles of digital citizenship outlined in this agreement and accept that failing to follow these tenets will have consequences.

Signed: _____ Date: _____ / _____ / _____

References and Resources

1951 British Mount Everest reconnaissance expedition. (n.d.). In *Wikipedia*. Accessed at https://en.wikipedia.org/wiki/1951_British_Mount_Everest_reconnaissance_expedition on March 27, 2017.

Amoros, R. (2015, November 4). *The US spends $35 billion on foreign aid . . . but where does the money really go?* Accessed at http://mondoweiss.net/2015/11/spends-billion-foreign on January 16, 2017.

Anderson, L. W., & Krathwohl, D. (Eds.). (2001). *A taxonomy for learning, teaching, and assessing: A revision of Bloom's taxonomy of educational objectives*. New York: Longman.

Australian Curriculum. (n.d.a). *General capabilities: Introduction*. Accessed at www.australiancurriculum.edu.au/generalcapabilities/overview/introduction on July 24, 2016.

Australian Curriculum. (n.d.b). *Intercultural understanding*. Accessed at www.australiancurriculum.edu.au/generalcapabilities/intercultural-understanding/introduction/introduction on May 4, 2017.

Blitzer, R. J., Petersen, C., & Rodgers, L. (1993, February). How to build self-esteem. *Training & Development*, 58–60. Accessed at http://go.galegroup.com/ps/anonymous?id=GALE%7CA13975358&sid=googleScholar&v=2.1&it=r&linkaccess=fulltext&issn=10559760&p=AONE&sw=w&authCount=1&isAnonymousEntry=true on May 21, 2017.

Bloom's digital taxonomy. (n.d.). In *Educational Origami*. Accessed at http://edorigami.wikispaces.com/Bloom%27s+Digital+Taxonomy on February 23, 2017.

Bradner, E. (2016, September 8). *Personal brawls dominate 2016 race*. Accessed at www.cnn.com/2016/09/08/politics/trump-clinton-policy-free-2016-election on January 16, 2017.

Bring your own device. (n.d.). In *Wikipedia*. Accessed at https://en.wikipedia.org/wiki/Bring_your_own_device on January 9, 2017.

Center for Climate and Energy Solutions. (n.d.). *Main greenhouse gases*. Accessed at www.c2es.org/facts-figures/main-ghgs on January 16, 2017.

Chambers, C. (2013, August 12). Psychology's answer to trolling and online abuse. *The Guardian*. Accessed at www.theguardian.com/science/head-quarters/2013/aug/12/psychology-trolling-online-abuse on June 1, 2017.

Cisco. (2016, June). *The zettabyte era—Trends and analysis*. San Jose, CA: Author. Accessed at www.cisco.com/c/en/us/solutions/collateral/service-provider/visual-networking-index -vni/vni-hyperconnectivity-wp.html on January 16, 2017.

Common Sense Media. (n.d.). *Facebook, Instagram, and social*. Accessed at www .commonsensemedia.org/social-media on January 16, 2017.

Creative Commons. (n.d.). *What is Creative Commons?* Accessed at https://wiki.creativecommons .org/images/3/35/Creativecommons-what-is-creative-commons_eng.pdf on February 21, 2017.

Crockett, L. W. (2016, August 23). *How to search and attribute open source images the right way*. Accessed at https://globaldigitalcitizen.org/search-attribute-open-source-images on June 1, 2017.

Crockett, L. W. (2017, February 8). *Teaching global digital citizenship? Use these 10 essential questions*. Accessed at https://globaldigitalcitizen.org/teaching-global-digital-citizenship -10-essential-questions on June 1, 2017.

Crockett, L. W., & Churches, A. (2017). *Mindful assessment: The 6 essential fluencies of innovative learning*. Bloomington, IN: Solution Tree Press.

Crockett, L. W., Jukes, I., & Churches, A. (2011). *Literacy is not enough: 21st-century fluencies for the digital age*. Thousand Oaks, CA: Corwin Press.

D'Alessandro, N. (2014, April 7). 22 facts about plastic pollution (and 10 things we can do about it). *EcoWatch*. Accessed at www.ecowatch.com/22-facts-about-plastic-pollution -and-10-things-we-can-do-about-it-1881885971.html on June 1, 2017.

Dweck, C. S. (2006). *Mindset: The new psychology of success*. New York: Random House.

E, J. (2016, September 2). *2016 may be hottest year yet: Global warming at an 'unprecedented' pace in a millenium* [sic]*, NASA says*. Accessed at www.natureworldnews.com/articles /27988/20160902/2016-hottest-year-global-warming-unprecedented-pace -millenium-nasa.htm on January 16, 2017.

Edmund Hillary. (n.d.). In *Wikipedia*. Accessed at https://en.wikipedia.org/wiki/Edmund _Hillary on March 27, 2017.

Eisenstark, R. (2015, May 29). China's rural dumping grounds. *Slate*. Accessed at www.slate .com/articles/life/caixin/2015/05/china_s_waste_management_garbage_disposal_in _the_country_s_rural_areas_is.html on January 16, 2017.

Erikson's stages of psychosocial development. (n.d.). In *Wikipedia*. Accessed at https:// en.wikipedia.org/wiki/Erikson%27s_stages_of_psychosocial_development on January 9, 2017.

Frontline/World. (2009, June 23). *Ghana: Digital dumping ground* [Video file]. Accessed at www .pbs.org/frontlineworld/stories/ghana804/video/video_index.html on January 16, 2017.

Getty. (n.d.). China's electronic waste village. *Time*. Accessed at http://content.time.com/time /photogallery/0,29307,1870162,00.html on January 16, 2017.

Graber, D. (2016a, April 15). *Internet safety education: 10 questions parents should be asking* [Blog post]. Accessed at www.huffingtonpost.com/diana-graber/internet-safety -education_b_9695250.html on January 16, 2017.

Graber, D. (2016b, February 5). *"What if's" surrounding social media's role in Nicole Lovell's death* [Blog post]. Accessed at www.huffingtonpost.com/diana-graber/what-ifs -surrounding-soci_b_9162348.html on January 16, 2017.

Gunning fog index. (n.d.). In *Wikipedia*. Accessed at https://en.wikipedia.org/wiki/Gunning _fog_index on January 9, 2017.

Harmful Digital Communications Act 2015, Pub. A. No. 63 (2015).

Hassan, C. (2016, March 31). Is the streaming industry lying about piracy? *Digital Music News*. Accessed at www.digitalmusicnews.com/2016/03/31/is-streaming-making-piracyworse on January 16, 2017.

Huppert, B. (2015, April 20). 700,000 sandwiches later, this man is still helping the homeless. *USA Today*. Accessed at www.usatoday.com/story/news/2015/04/20/inspiration -nation-sandwich-man/26096691 on January 16, 2017.

IDEAS for Global Citizenship. (n.d.). *What is global citizenship?* Accessed at www.ideas-forum .org.uk/about-us/global-citizenship on January 16, 2017.

In loco parentis. (n.d.). In *Wikipedia*. Accessed at https://en.wikipedia.org/wiki/In_loco_parentis on January 9, 2017.

International Baccalaureate. (2014). *Approaches to teaching and learning in the International Baccalaureate (IB) Diploma Programme*. Accessed at www.ibo.org/globalassets/digital -tookit/flyers-and-artworks/approaches-to-teaching-learning-dp-en.pdf on January 9, 2017.

International Baccalaureate. (2015, June). *What is an IB education?* Cardiff, Wales: Author. Accessed at www.ibo.org/globalassets/digital-tookit/brochures/what-is-an-ib -education-en.pdf on January 16, 2017.

International Society for Technology in Education. (2008). *ISTE standards for teachers*. Accessed at www.iste.org/standards/standards/standards-for-teachers on July 31, 2017.

International Union for Conservation of Nature. (2016, September 6). *Latest ocean warming review reveals extent of impacts on nature and humans*. Accessed at www.sciencedaily .com/releases/2016/09/160906085016.htm on January 16, 2017.

Johnstone, B. (2003). *Never mind the laptops: Kids, computers, and the transformation of learning*. New York: iUniverse.

Karmatube. (n.d.). *The sandwich man* [Video file]. Accessed at www.karmatube.org/videos .php?id=5975 on January 16, 2017.

Kline, T. (n.d.). *Are we teaching responsibility or just obedience?* Accessed at www.changekidslives .org/thoughts-2 on June 1, 2017.

Knowles, M. S. (1980). *The modern practice of adult education: From pedagogy to andragogy* (Rev. ed.). Wilton, CT: Association Press.

Kohlberg, L. (2008). The development of children's orientations toward a moral order. *Human Development, 51*(8), 8–20.

Lanaria, V. (2016, January 5). *Top 10 most common digital piracy myths busted: Who's pirating what and why?* Accessed at www.techtimes.com/articles/121118/20160105/top-10 -most-common-digital-piracy-myths-busted-who-s-pirating-what-and-why.htm on January 16, 2017.

Learning and Work Institute England. (n.d.). *SMOG calculator*. Accessed at www.niace.org.uk /misc/SMOG-calculator/smogcalc.php# on January 16, 2017.

Li, J. (2015, February 1). *Ways forward from China's urban waste problem*. Accessed at https:// thenatureofcities.com/2015/02/01/ways-forward-from-chinas-urban-waste-problem on January 16, 2017.

Ma, L., Montgomery, A., & Smith, M. D. (2016, February 24). *The dual impact of movie piracy on box-office revenue: Cannibalization and promotion.* Accessed at https://ssrn.com/abstract=2736946 on March 27, 2017.

Magid, L. (2013, June 3). A third of recently married couples met online and they're more satisfied and less likely to split-up. *Forbes.* Accessed at www.forbes.com/sites/larrymagid/2013/06/03/a-third-of-recently-married-couples-met-online-and-theyre-more-satisfied-and-less-likely-to-split-up/#3557bf65595e on May 21, 2017.

Maps of World. (2016, June 1). *Top ten donors of foreign aid.* Accessed at www.mapsofworld.com/world-top-ten/world-top-ten-doners-of-foreigner-aid-map.html on January 16, 2017.

McElvaney, K. (2014, February 27). Agbogbloshie: The world's largest e-waste dump—in pictures. *The Guardian.* Accessed at www.theguardian.com/environment/gallery/2014/feb/27/agbogbloshie-worlds-largest-e-waste-dump-in-pictures on January 16, 2017.

McGilvery, C. (2012). Promoting responsible and ethical digital citizens. *Education World.* Accessed at www.educationworld.com/a_tech/responsible-student-technology-use.shtml on January 16, 2017.

Minneapolis Recreation Development. (n.d.). *MRD founder Mr. Allan Law.* Accessed at www.363days.org/allanlaw.html on January 16, 2017.

Minter, A. (2015, June 16). *Anatomy of a myth: The world's biggest e-waste dump isn't* [Blog post]. Accessed at http://shanghaiscrap.com/2015/06/anatomy-of-a-myth-the-worlds-biggest-e-waste-dump-isnt on January 16, 2017.

Molla, R., & Ovide, S. (2016, March 23). *The war on Internet piracy.* Accessed at www.bloomberg.com/gadfly/articles/2016-03-23/google-and-media-titans-clash-in-a-war-on-internet-piracy on January 16, 2017.

Morris, W. (2015, November 2). *China's growing consumer waste challenge.* Accessed at www.coresponsibility.com/china-and-consumer-waste on January 16, 2017.

Morrison, S. (2014, March 21). The majority of international aid is not reaching the countries that need it the most. *Independent.* Accessed at www.independent.co.uk/news/world/africa/the-majority-of-international-aid-is-not-reaching-the-countries-that-need-it-the-most-9206182.html on January 16, 2017.

New Zealand Ministry of Education. (n.d.). *Cultural diversity.* Accessed at http://nzcurriculum.tki.org.nz/Principles/Cultural-diversity on May 4, 2017.

New Zealand Ministry of Education. (2007). *The New Zealand curriculum.* Wellington, New Zealand: Learning Media Limited. Accessed at http://nzcurriculum.tki.org.nz/The-New-Zealand-Curriculum on May 4, 2017.

Online Utility. (n.d.). *Tests document readability: Readability calculator.* Accessed at www.online-utility.org/english/readability_test_and_improve.jsp on August 27, 2016.

Pacific Institute. (2007). *Bottled water and energy fact sheet.* Accessed at http://pacinst.org/publication/bottled-water-and-energy-a-fact-sheet on June 1, 2017.

Patchin, J. W. (2011, February 10). *When can educators search student cell phones?* Accessed at http://cyberbullying.org/when-can-educators-search-student-cell-phones on June 1, 2017.

Popper, B., & Erlick, N. (2017, February 1). *Facebook is closing in on 2 billion monthly users.* Accessed at www.theverge.com/2017/2/1/14474534/facebook-earnings-q4-fourth-quarter-2016 on April 19, 2017.

PR Newswire. (2016, August 2). *Flex releases 2016 Global Citizenship Report.* Accessed at http://finance.yahoo.com/news/flex-releases-2016-global-citizenship-201500064.html on January 16, 2017.

Reimers, F. M. (2016a, July 21). *Empowering global citizens to improve the world* [Blog post]. Accessed at www.huffingtonpost.com/fernando-reimers/empowering-global-citizen_b_11099352.html on January 9, 2017.

Reimers, F. M. (2016b, July 29). Turning students into global citizens. *Education Week.* Accessed at www.edweek.org/ew/articles/2016/08/03/turning-students-into-global-citizens.html on January 16, 2017.

ScienceDaily. (n.d.). *Global warming.* Accessed at www.sciencedaily.com/terms/global_warming.htm on January 9, 2017.

Seiff, J. (2016, March 13). *Time to assess the true cost of digital piracy, says Winnipeg author.* Accessed at www.cbc.ca/news/canada/manitoba/time-to-reconsider-the-cost-digital-piracy-1.3488270 on January 16, 2017.

Shibata, M. (2015, June 11). *Inside the world's biggest e-waste dump.* Accessed at http://motherboard.vice.com/read/inside-the-worlds-biggest-e-waste-dump on January 16, 2017.

Sim, M. (2015, June 25). *(UPDATE) Transforming Agbogbloshie: From toxic dump into model recycling center* [Blog post]. Accessed at www.pureearth.org/blog/photos-transforming-agbogbloshie-from-toxic-e-waste-dump-into-model-recycling-center on January 16, 2017.

SINTEF. (2013, May 22). Big data, for better or worse: 90% of world's data generated over last two years. *ScienceDaily.* Accessed at www.sciencedaily.com/releases/2013/05/130522085217.htm on September 9, 2016.

SMOG. (n.d.). In *Wikipedia.* Accessed at https://en.wikipedia.org/wiki/SMOG on January 9, 2017.

Starnes, T. (2016, August 18). SHOCKING! School makes kids take personal responsibility! *Fox News.* Accessed at www.foxnews.com/opinion/2016/08/18/shocking-school-makes-kids-take-personal-responsibility.html on January 16, 2017.

Statista. (n.d.a). *Number of apps available in leading app stores as of June 2016.* Accessed at www.statista.com/statistics/276623/number-of-apps-available-in-leading-app-stores on August 16, 2016.

Statista. (n.d.b). *Number of available applications in the Google Play store from December 2009 to December 2016.* Accessed at www.statista.com/statistics/266210/number-of-available-applications-in-the-google-play-store on August 16, 2016.

StopBullying.gov. (n.d.). *Effects of bullying.* Accessed at www.stopbullying.gov/at-risk/effects/index.html on May 21, 2017.

Swanson, A. (2015, October 23). *Does foreign aid always help the poor?* Accessed at www.weforum.org/agenda/2015/10/does-foreign-aid-always-help-the-poor on January 16, 2017.

Te Kete Ipurangi. (2014, April 4). *Key competencies.* Accessed at http://nzcurriculum.tki.org.nz/Key-competencies on July 23, 2016.

TopTenSM Staff. (n.d.). *10 pros and cons of social media.* Accessed at www.toptensocialmedia.com/social-media-social-buzz/10-pros-and-cons-of-social-media on January 16, 2017.

Upadhyaya, V. (2016, August 9). *Why startup founders ought to be global citizens.* Accessed at https://inc42.com/entrepreneurship/startup-founders-global-citizens on January 16, 2017.

United States Environmental Protection Agency. (n.d.). *Global greenhouse gas emissions data.* Accessed at www.epa.gov/ghgemissions/global-greenhouse-gas-emissions-data on January 16, 2017.

USA.gov. (n.d.). *Presidential election process.* Accessed at www.usa.gov/election on January 16, 2017.

US-China Business Council. (2016, April 6). *Trash or treasure? Prospects for China's recycling industry.* Accessed at www.chinabusinessreview.com/trash-or-treasure-prospects-for-chinas-recycling-industry on January 16, 2017.

Vanderklippe, N. (2015, May 11). China's trash is taking over. *Globe and Mail.* Accessed at www.theglobeandmail.com/news/world/chinas-trash-is-taking-over/article24367032 on January 16, 2017.

Vick, K. (2015, May 27). Most foreign aid does not go to neediest countries, report finds. *Time.* Accessed at http://time.com/3897960/foreign-aid-poor-countries-extreme-poverty on January 16, 2017.

Vitrium. (2014). *No big deal? Copyright and piracy online* [Infographic]. Accessed at www.vitrium.com/media/images/no-big-deal-copyright-piracy-online.jpg on January 16, 2017.

Welch, C. (2017, June 27). Facebook crosses 2 billion monthly users. *The Verge.* Accessed at www.theverge.com/2017/6/27/15880494/facebook-2-billion-monthly-users-announced on July 3, 2017.

Wiggins, G., & McTighe, J. (2005). *Understanding by design* (Expanded 2nd ed.). Alexandria, VA: Association for Supervision and Curriculum Development.

Woollaston, V. (2014, September 17). Number of websites hits a BILLION: Tracker reveals a new site is registered every SECOND. *Daily Mail.* Accessed at www.dailymail.co.uk/sciencetech/article-2759636/Number-websites-hits-BILLION-counting-Tracker-reveals-new-site-registered-SECOND.html on August 16, 2016.

World Wide Web Consortium. (2016). *Tim Berners-Lee: Biography.* Accessed at www.w3.org/People/Berners-Lee on January 9, 2017.

YaleGlobal Online. (n.d.). *US election and the world.* Accessed at http://yaleglobal.yale.edu/special-reports/us-election-world on January 16, 2017.

Zhang, J.W. & Chen, S. (2016, January 20). Self-compassion promotes personal improvement from regret experiences. *Acceptance, 42*(2), 244–258. Accessed at http://journals.sagepub.com/doi/pdf/10.1177/0146167215623271 on June 1, 2017.

Index

Mindful Assessment

Lee Watanabe Crockett and Andrew Churches

It is time to rethink the relationship between teaching and learning and assess the crucial skills students need to succeed in the 21st century. Educators must focus assessment on mindfulness and feedback, framing assessment around six fluencies students need to cultivate.

BKF717

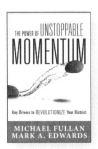

The Power of Unstoppable Momentum

Michael Fullan and Mark A. Edwards

Your school district can revolutionize its culture to improve student learning. This book details a simple but powerful process for integrating technology, pedagogy, and deep learning that leads to lasting change. Included are real examples of districts that attained pedagogically driven, digitally accelerated success.

BKF701

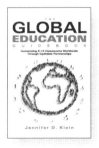

The Global Education Guidebook

Jennifer D. Klein

Educators worldwide are striving to connect students to classrooms and experts, to humanize the world while preparing them to thrive in the 21st century. This practical guide shares steps and strategies to set up equitable global partnerships that benefit all learners.

BKF763

Reimagining Literacy Through Global Collaboration

Pernille Ripp

This how-to guide provides strategies for establishing classrooms that give students globally connected literacy experiences. Discover how to create environments where students gain 21st century skills, realize that their work matters, and know that their work travels beyond classroom walls.

BKF732

Wait! Your professional development journey doesn't have to end with the last pages of this book.

We realize improving student learning doesn't happen overnight. And your school or district shouldn't be left to puzzle out all the details of this process alone.

No matter where you are on the journey, we're committed to helping you get to the next stage.

Take advantage of everything from **custom workshops** to **keynote presentations** and **interactive web and video conferencing**. We can even help you develop an action plan tailored to fit your specific needs.

Let's get the conversation started.

Call 888.763.9045 today.

SolutionTree.com